How to
Love
&
Be Loved

establishing and maintaining intimacy

D0911761

How to
Love
&
Be Loved

establishing and maintaining intimacy

By Richard A. Osing

A Consortium Corporation Book

Rudi Publishing
Iowa City, Iowa

Rudi Publishing, 1901 Broadway, Suite 321, Iowa City,
Iowa 52240

Distributed to the trade in the United States by:
The Consortium Corporation
200 Fifth Avenue S.E.
P.O. Box 2419
Cedar Rapids, Iowa 52406
319-399-6901 • 1-800-999-6901

Library of Congress Cataloging-in-Publication Data
92-061144

ISBN 0-945213-05-0

First Edition, October 1992

PRINTED IN THE UNITED STATES OF AMERICA

♥ Dedication

This book is dedicated to my paternal grand-mother, Annie Osing, and to my wife, Jo.

These are the two women who have enriched my life the most. Grandma truly ordained me to the ministry. Jo helped me to heal from some of the wounds of that ministry.

Contents

Acknowledgments

Any author is indebted to many people who stand behind a book as invisible contributors, and I am no exception.

I am indeed indebted to many persons over the years who entrusted me with their pain and their problems. I learned about loving by listening to them.

I am indebted to my wife, who encouraged me and supported this effort in so many ways. Likewise, to my children, Mark, Matthew, and Mary, for their love and support always, even when times were not the happiest. Also to my stepchildren, Steve and Anne, who many times urged me to "go for it."

I am particularly indebted to Dr. Vernon Varner, M.D., J.D., for his encouragement. He invited me to join his psychiatric practice in 1986 and thereby gave me the opportunity to expand my knowledge and experience. I have also been enriched by my colleagues at the clinic: Mary Varner, L.S.W., Janet Smith Shepherd, Ph.D., and Darlene Parr, M.A. Our staff meetings on Friday mornings have been a delight.

My stepson, Steve Fairchild, has put in many hours of work with his partner, Tom Leidigh. Because of them I have been unburdened of any of the many business details which are part of this kind of endeavor.

In addition, I am grateful to my editor, Nancy Ewald, and publisher, Terri Boekhoff. They nudged me to make changes and additions which have greatly improved the final product. Both of them assured me

I could write when I was convinced that the truth was otherwise.

I want to acknowledge the assistance of Mary Gardner, Sandy Paulson, and Linda Hobart for the special typing they have done for me. All three have done a great job deciphering my handwriting.

Finally, I am appreciative of Mindy Hoeppner's timely assistance in tracking down song titles.

Chapter 1

Too Much Love—
Not Many Lovers

Ask ten people on the street what they want out of life, what they want in the future, and eight out of ten will use some form of the word *happiness*. "Don't Worry—Be Happy" was a popular novelty song in 1989.[1] The problem is discovering what ingredients one needs to have in one's life in order to be happy. Happiness is really very elusive. We soon discover that a lot of things which we think will bring us happiness do not. The wisest minds, in fact, suggest that happiness is not so much *having* anything. Happiness is more like a by-product of living than the result of the direct search for something.

I believe that, at least in a general way, I can suggest two areas of life that seem to hold the keys to the experiencing of happiness. To be happy, you need to have satisfying experiences in two areas: First, you need to be doing something with your life that you believe is worthwhile. You need to experience the satisfaction of accomplishing something with your life. And second, you need to experience the satisfaction of a loving relationship with at least one person. It is to be hoped that you will have that relationship with more than one, but one is the minimum.

My attempt to delineate what makes for happiness is very minimal. I have said nothing about money. I don't think money in itself brings happiness. Nor have I said anything about education. I don't think knowledge in itself brings happiness. But the experience of a loving relationship and the accomplishment

---

1. Bobby McFarrin, "Don't Worry—Be Happy," 1988

of something worthwhile in themselves seem to be associated with happiness.

In this book I would like to elaborate on just one of these areas: loving relationships. I do so fully aware that the world is not particularly lacking in books on the subject. So why another book? Frankly, the answer is that while I have read many books on the subject and have been impressed with many of them, I haven't read some of the things that I have learned, both through my own personal struggle with love and in my counseling with couples. These ideas I would like to share in the hope that they will give you, the reader, another view that may be helpful in your own relationships.

Love is not a trivial pursuit in America. By my own rough estimate, eight of every ten songs we sing are about love—love celebrated, love gone wrong, love unrequited, etc. Loving relationships are the focus of most television programs, and not just the "soaps." Danielle Steele has become a household name and Harlequin romances a part of every American drugstore. But the continuing appetite reveals that somehow we haven't uncovered the secret of love. We are still searching.

It is part of our American ethos that love and marriage are inexorably linked. The majority opinion is that the link is positive, that is, love leads to marriage and marriage is the natural arena for the sharing and the multiplying of love. We used to sing a song that went, "love and marriage go together like a horse and carriage" and, later in the verse, "you can't have one without the other." So you can't have "love" without getting married and you can't have "marriage" unless there is love. That's what we affirm in America.

Lots of folks would agree with the notion that you can't have love without marriage. There has been for some time a protesting minority that has believed that not only is love possible without marriage, but that something about marriage itself destroys love. So we have had several decades now when living together without marriage has been popular. The practice is now in decline because people have discovered that the rationale for living together without marriage was not true. Marriage does not destroy love.

But something certainly does seem to destroy love *and* marriage in the same process. At this writing (Summer, 1991) there are 3,000 divorces per day in America.[2] And since each divorce involves one husband, one wife, and an average of one child, that means 9,000 people per day are being painfully affected by divorce. And the numbers cited do not take into consideration grandparents and other extended family members.

The divorce figures also indicate that for all of our interest in love, for all our songs, our soaps, our movies, and our books, we are having trouble "finding" love, or having once "found" it, cannot seem to maintain it. The wonder is that we keep looking. It says something about human persistence that the overwhelming majority of people do not give up in the quest for love. There must be something quite funda-

---

2. Martin Textor, ed., *The Divorce and Divorce Therapy Handbook* (Northvale, NJ: J. Aronson Inc., 1989) preface viii.

mental about the make-up of human beings that will not allow us, except at great cost, to deny our need for love. The evidence is convincing that we do have, in the words of Bill Glasser, a "genetic instruction" to love and be loved.[3]

Another wonder is that, for all the cultural attention on love, the subject never seems to get priority concern in the American school system. I find it a curious anomaly that the majority of American youth graduate from high school (singing the songs, watching the TV programs, seeing the movies—all about love) without ever being exposed to some serious reflection about love. (I'll explain why this anomaly exists later.)

I know that there are some courses in some high schools with titles such as "Marriage and Family Living." A few of them are outstanding courses taught by creative and dedicated professionals. I also know that introductory psychology (or sociology) courses contain some chapters on marriage and child rearing. But my observation still stands: The majority of youth who are dating and experimenting with "love" and sometimes making choices of a husband or wife are not exposed to serious reflection about love and loving relationships.

Yet I can assure you they are interested in the subject. I know that they are because it is one of the great joys of my life to be invited to talk to high school people about love. I have experienced one hundred

3. William Glasser, *Control Theory* (New York: Harper and Row, 1984)

high school students sitting still and being quiet enough to hear a pin drop. Some of their teachers were amazed. They flattered me with their compliments but, frankly, I knew it wasn't really I who got that attention—it was the subject. I was talking about something they were really interested in. The interest was already there. I did not have to motivate them at all. Young people have lots of questions about love. They experience much psychic pain, and even commit suicide over failed relationships.

Most college students are not exposed to serious reflection about love either. Leo Buscaglia's courses at the University of Southern California are the exception, not the rule.[4] Again, perhaps some psychology majors or people taking counseling courses do delve into the subject, but we are talking about a minority. What most college students learn about love they learn in bull sessions, frequently centered around TV programs, some fraternity brother's break-up with his girlfriend, or a sorority group discussion about why men are so stupid when it comes to women.

My point? It's simple. Americans who believe that love is what makes a marriage work do not seem to take the time to seriously reflect on or teach people how to do *loving*. We can sing about it, dramatize it, and "humorize" it, and yet manage never really to confront head-on the question, "How do you love another person?"

Imagine the typical sixteen-year-old who walks into a drivers' licensing office and asks for a license on

---

4. Leo Buscaglia, *Love* (Greenwich: Fawcett, 1972)

the grounds of having reached the appropriate age. "You do not get a license just because you are sixteen," the youth will be told. "First, you must demonstrate that you have learned something about automobile operation. You must have taken a semester of Driver's Ed, or at least have read your state's version of the auto driver's manual." In either case, it does require some minimal intellectual effort. But not *just* that. Driving a car, after all, involves a set of skills, and before most states will give you a license, you will have to demonstrate that you have sufficiently mastered those skills. Only then will you be licensed to drive.

Now imagine two such youths, a male and female, just two years later. They are in the county clerk's office requesting a marriage license. They are about to embark on an endeavor that involves a lot more skills than driving a car. But without ever having read a paragraph on the subject of love or parenthood, without being expected to demonstrate any of the skills involved in loving, communicating, problem solving, or any other related skills, they will be given a license. Assured of their undying love for each other, they will go off with their license totally unprepared for the task of loving and making a marriage work. And half of them will be divorced.

How about the premarital counseling done by clergy? Most clergy take their responsibility quite seriously. Some brave souls adamantly refuse to perform the ceremony if the couple will not attend counseling sessions. Many clergy are well trained for this work and use some good material. But at the risk of offending some of my brothers and sisters of the cloth, I'm afraid the net results are often very minimal. The best that happens is that a relationship is established between the couple and the minister, priest, or rabbi, so the couple will come back when there is a problem. There are two problems with premarital counseling. The first problem is that it is too late. Choices have been made, the invitations have been ordered, the reception hall has been booked. The man and woman are "sure" of their undying love for each other, so the clergyman or clergywoman who is moved by conscience to confront some obvious obstacles risks judgments about his or her competence.

The second problem is that the couple is not really thinking "marriage," but instead thinking "wedding." These are not the same thing. Profound differences in the way two people look at life, at money, or at religion are seen only as obstacles that threaten to make the *wedding* difficult. A couple once came to me to inquire my "price" for performing a wedding. These young people were concerned that they could not afford a church wedding. I asked them how they could afford rent and groceries for the next month, and they looked at me in astonishment. "How can you afford marriage?" I asked. Another couple sought my counsel because each set of parents had vowed to boycott the wedding if it was held in the other's church. It never occurred to this couple that this significant religious antagonism would be a problem *after* the wedding.

So there you have it. Americans insist that a loving relationship is the necessary prerequisite to a happy,

fulfilling marriage, and that a continuing loving relationship is necessary for the marriage to endure. But
strangely, we are doing too little too late, if anything
at all, to teach people *how to do the kind of loving* that
will sustain a marriage through all the stages of
married life.

Now occasionally there are some legislators or
jurists (or religious people) who also get upset at the
frightful cost paid by men, women, and children
because of the trauma of divorce and broken homes.
And frequently, as these concerned people cast about
for something or someone to blame, their glances fall
on the divorce laws of the country. "It's too easy to get
a divorce," they say. I categorically disagree with that
point of view. It is *not* too easy to get a divorce.
Nobody who has ever been through one (as I have)
will tell you it is easy. It is, in fact, an agonizing,
traumatic experience fraught with guilt, feelings of
abandonment, despair, uncertainty, and pain that lasts
for a long time. Judith Wallerstein has published the
evidence that divorce has effects on adults and
children that last much longer than we have as-
sumed.[5] Let no one say it is too easy to get a divorce.
It isn't.

Nor is the problem a matter of people just
thinking they are in love, not being mature enough, or
having some romantic notions that blind them to
reality. All of the above have happened. But the real
truth is that most people at the time of their wedding

5. Judith Wallerstein, et al, *Surviving the Breakup* (New York:
Harper Torch Books, 1980)

are sincerely convinced that their relationship will endure for a lifetime. Most couples have a relationship that is reality oriented and fairly loving. So why the rate of failure? My answer is that our rate of marital failure is due in part to our unwillingness to seriously and conscientiously teach people how to establish and maintain loving relationships. It is our unwillingness to demand more from people *before* we issue them a marriage license. It is our failure to see that if we demand that marriages be maintained by love, then we must do much more to teach people about that kind of love, how to establish it, and how to maintain it.

Before I get to what I think should be taught, let me say that I do not want to give the impression that in the absence of any formal teaching or disciplined reflection on love people in America grow up without any notions about love. Quite the contrary. It is impossible to grow up in America without learning quite a bit about love. But what do we learn, and how do we learn it?

Chapter Two

❤

What You Learn about Love Growing Up in America

There are really three different sources for our "learning" about love and marriage. One comes after the wedding and two before. What we learn from personal experience comes after the wedding. And many people do learn a lot about love and marriage in the process of being married. Sometimes that learning serves to improve the quality of a marriage. Sometimes what we learn persuades us to leave a marriage.

One major source of learning about love and marriage before the wedding is the marriage each of us grows up in—that of our parents. That learning is indeed quite powerful, even if it is mostly unconscious. As a child growing up we each seldom look critically at our parents' marriage. We live in it daily, however, and our eye-brain videos are taking thousands of little pictures as Mom and Dad model for us how to be a woman/man, wife/husband, and mother/father.

These pictures or images become part of the basis of our own expectations of ourselves and our spouses. Unless we consciously avoid someone like Mom or Dad because we were personally hurt by the way that parent played that role, we each expect to play a role quite similar to our same-sex parent's and to expect that our spouse will play a role similar to our opposite-sex parent's.

And more. We also interact as persons with our parents. And the patterns of those interactions take on great importance for our later interpersonal dynamics. These dynamics have a way of exerting a powerful influence on our choice of lovers. It is generally agreed today that we are unconsciously attracted to persons with whom we can re-create the important emotional issue(s) of childhood so that we can resolve in our marriage what was not resolved in childhood.

I refer to the family-of-origin issue here because it is so important for most people. Other authors, such as Hendrix,[1] have done an outstanding job in spelling out the crucial importance of childhood models.

A second source of learning about love and marriage before the wedding, a source which is also a powerful influence on our notions of love and marriage, is the *cultural images, models, and messages*. Even more so than in our families, learning about love in the cultural arena is unconscious. Yet the learning we do is quite powerful—perhaps just because it is unconscious. We sing or hum the songs of our culture, enjoying the melody, the beat, or the harmony. What we normally do *not* do is critically analyze the words of the song. We have watched years of "I Love Lucy," "The Honeymooners," "The Brady Bunch," "Leave It To Beaver," "Hill Street Blues," "L.A. Law," "Dallas," and on and on—television sitcoms and dramas and serials which are saturated with portrayals of love relationships and marriage. Through it all—the songs, the TV portrayals, the movies, the romance novels—it seems to me there are some common threads, the weaving together of a "love mystique" that is uniquely American. My very limited work with people from other societies teaches me that they do

---

1. Harville Hendrix, *Getting the Love You Want* (New York: Henry Holt and Company, 1988)

not grow up with the same notions that we do. They do have some notions of their own that are just as destructive. But they do not learn what we learn about love in America.

Five notions seem to stand out as parts of the American "love mystique."

Notion One: Love belongs to the realm of mystery and magic and is therefore known intuitively.

"What is this thing called love? This funny thing called love? Who can solve its *mystery?* Why does it make a fool of me?"[2]

"Ah sweet *mystery* of life at last I've found you."[3]

"Don't take nothing to make love come to you, but it takes *magic* to make it stay."[4]

"You sigh the song begins; You speak and I hear violins. It's *magic.*"[5]

"Come feel the *magic* between you and I. I've got hungry eyes."[6]

The above songs come quickly to mind. There are many more—all persuading us to assign the experi-

---

2. Cole Porter, "What Is This Thing Called Love?" 1929

3. Victor Herbert and Rida Young, "Ah Sweet Mystery of Life," 1910

4. "Ain't No Trick—It Takes Magic," MCA recording #MCA-52150, 1982

5. Sammy Cahn and Julie Styne, "It's Magic," 1948

6. Allen and O'Brien, "Hungry Eyes," 1988

ence of love to the realm of mystery and magic.

So how can I tell whether my relationship with a particular person will make me "feel the magic?" The American "love mystique" answers, "Don't worry. You'll *just know*." This notion easily encourages us to confuse sexual arousal with love. We may be even a little irritated at Masters and Johnson for "taking out the magic" by hooking people up to all those machines to measure such things as heart rate and blood pressure, because in America it is considered that true love is signaled by the intuitive awareness of a mysterious and magical connection.

Notion Two: Love is an experience outside of human control.

You will object that you have never heard a song which affirmed anything so silly as that. But in fact you have probably heard hundreds of such songs. In America the most frequently used expression for the onset of a loving relationship is "falling." We "fall" in love.

Think about that term. Into what kind of philosophical category would you put it? I'll tell you. It belongs under the classification of *accident*. Falling is, after all, an accident; something I do because I am momentarily careless; and, most important, something for which I bear no—or at least diminished—responsibility. "I couldn't help it, I fell," is what your six-year-old tells you when he shows up with a major grass stain on his brand new pants. And that's pre-

cisely how we are encouraged to think about love—
as an accident over which we have no—or at least
limited—control.

"I cain't help it; I just fell in love with you."[7]

"You made me love you, I didn't want to do it."[8]

The latter song line suggests that someone could
make us love *against our will.* I have occasionally had
an anguished spouse or lover in my office who has
pleaded with me, "Please make her (him) love me
again." So in America we are encouraged to think of
love as an accident over which we have little or no
control; perhaps even as something which could
happen *to* us contrary to our own will.

Notion Three: The secret to a loving relationship is finding *the person* who is *right* for you.

"You were meant for me. I was meant for you."[9]

"It's sad to belong to someone else when 'the right
one' comes along."[10]

"I just don't think we're right for each other," is the
kind of thing men and women say to each other to
soften the blow of rejection. It avoids the truth: "I don't

---

7. Hank Williams, "I Cain't Help It," 1951

8. Joe McCarthy and James Monaco, "You Made Me Love
You," 1939

9. Arthur Freed and Herb Brown, "You Were Meant for Me,"
1929

10. England Dan and John Ford Coley, "It's Sad to Belong,"
1977

love you." We have a strong desire to know *why* someone doesn't love us and the least hurtful rationale is "not right for each other." Nobody has to deal with some major fault or blame for hurting someone.

The flip side, however, is quite problematic. If I begin to feel quite unhappy in a relationship I am encouraged to think that the mistake I made was getting together with the wrong person. If this person were the "right one" we wouldn't be having all these problems.

------------------ 💛 ------------------

Notion Four: The key to Mr. (Ms.) Right is sexual compatibility.

In America we are encouraged to think that the key component (not the only one) in a love relationship is sexual compatibility. I am frequently asked to confirm the notion that marriages are made or broken in the bedroom. I would not want to give the impression that the sexual component of a relationship is not of central significance. It is. Its central importance does not get enough attention, in fact. The significance of the sexual component for the quality of the relationship throughout the life cycle of the relationship is crucial.

That is not what this notion of the love mystique says. It says that erotic compatibility is the key to which person is right for you, the key to love. Listen to Cher as she sings,

"How will you know if he loves you so? Is it in his eyes? No, No, No. Is it in the way he acts? No, No, No.

It's in his kiss—shoop, shoop, shoop!"[11]

In America we learn that the erotic quotient of a relationship is the way by which you identify "Mr. (Ms.) Right." It is the excitement of the kiss, the goose-bumps of the caress, the ecstasy of the orgasm—these tell you that someone is right for you, that you have found "true love."

Notion Five: Loving is something everybody knows how to do.

Given the fact that we have over 3,000 divorces a day in America[12] you would think that love, marriage, and family life would be a major concern of American education, at least beginning at the junior-high level. It is of some concern, but not of major concern. Here and there are some high-quality courses on marriage and family living—but my point in the previous chapter still stands: Most American youths are not exposed to serious reflection about love and its process in human living.

I believe that this is the case because such reflection is not considered necessary. Some people, I suppose, believe you can't tell people how to love—it's too mysterious or magical. But most, I suspect, believe it's not necessary because everybody knows "deep down" how to love. If we are in relationships in which we do not "feel loved" it is because some-

---

11. Clark, "The Shoop Shoop Song," 1964
12. Textor, *Divorce Handbook*

thing is wrong with our perception, or with our lovers' lousy commitments. It does not occur to us that we, or our lovers, or both, do not know how to love.

These are the five notions that combine to form the American "love mystique." These notions are continually reinforced in our culture—in songs, romance novels, television programs, and movies. I believe that they contribute to the tragic divorce statistics. They do so because all five of those notions are wrong.

Chapter 3

❤

The Truth about Love

Notion One was that love belongs to the realm of mystery and magic and is therefore "known" intuitively.

Truth One: Love is phenomenological and is "known" experientially.

It may be that the process of attraction is a little mysterious. Usually, though, the keys to why we are attracted to someone lie in our childhood experiences with the people who were our original caretakers. Either that, or with subsequent relationships in which we experienced pleasure. It may be that there is a depth to our humanness that has a mysterious quality.

But love is not mysterious. And it is not magical. You can "know" if your relationship is loving just as easily as you "know" what the temperature is outside, whether the wind is blowing, whether the broccoli casserole tastes good, or where the pain in your body is. You "know" because you are experiencing it or because you are not experiencing it.

Most people do know when they are not being well loved. And they usually say so. "You don't love me" is a charge frequently leveled by one person at another in a relationship. And that accusation arises from clear, unmistakable experiences of being neglected, abandoned, or abused. Your partner can complain, "but I do love you," but you "know" better because you are not experiencing loving.

Betty complains that Frank does not love her. Her complaint is based on her regular experience that his golfing schedule takes precedence over everything else during golfing season. Frank objects to the notion that he does not love Betty and insists he tells her that he loves her all the time. Yet he admits that Betty's observation about the priority of golf is essentially true. He cannot understand why Betty puts him in the position of having to choose between his love of golf and his love of her. He doesn't think of them as competing loves at all.

Both people in such situations are frequently hurt and confused about the other's feelings. Through the course of the next several chapters you will come to understand the reasons for this hurt and confusion. But make no mistake, loving is not mysterious or magical.

Notion Two was that love is outside of human control.

Truth Two: Love is completely under human control.

Notice that the difference between Notion Two and Truth Two is not just a matter of degree, nor is it just a misunderstanding, nor just a matter of definition. There is a categorical difference between them.

As indicated in the previous chapter, our culture sings and talks about love as though it is a matter of "falling," and falling in turn suggests that it is an accident. This is simply not true. We do not *fall* in love with anyone. The truth is we *decide* to love. And of course we may also decide not to love. We may, in fact, decide not to love someone we decided at some earlier time to love.

Loving is a volitional act. It is not accidental. Or, more accurately, loving requires a series of volitional acts. Every instance in the day-to-day mutual give and take of a relationship is a "moment of decision." In other words, deciding to love is not something I do just once or just periodically, but something I am doing, consciously or unconsciously, all the time. Every encounter I have with my beloved is potentially, at least, a moment of decision.

What happens that causes a decision to love to be changed into a decision not to love? How does one go from willing to love to refusing to love? The answer to that question is really complex, but let me give at least a partial explanation here. The decision to love or not to love is made on the basis of what I call "hinge experiences." A hinge is a gadget that a door swings on—either swings open or swings closed. Hinge experiences are the experiences on which the decision to love or not to love is based.

Ron and Mary Lou were doing fairly well in their suburban home. They had two children, two cars, and were thinking about a vacation cottage on a lake just three hours away. Mary Lou had worked full time when they were first married but quit her full-time job when the first baby was born. She was now earning some extra dollars doing day care for two other children. Ron had expected that Mary Lou would go back to a full-time job by the time their youngest was three. Their youngest was now four and Mary Lou kept putting off her search for full-time work. She did not want to go back to the office job she had worked at when they got married, and thought Ron would be satisfied if she earned the grocery money plus some extra. Besides, she really enjoyed the experience of being home all day.

Now, every time the subject came up Ron became more convinced that Mary Lou was not going to ever go back to work full time. He believed some of their financial goals could not be met if she did not get a full-time job. The arguments about money increased. Ron became conscious of a growing resentment toward his wife. He began to find himself more and more attracted to a female colleague doing the same work he did. They became friends. Eventually Ron separated from Mary Lou and filed for divorce. Mary Lou's unwillingness to meet Ron's expectation became the "hinge" on which he decided not to love her and to create an outside alliance.

Sometimes the hinge experience is just one colossal traumatic event like a husband coming home and finding his wife in bed with another man. Sometimes the hinge experience is really an accumulation over several years during which a particular hurt is experienced over and over again. Sometimes it is just an accumulation of disappointments because expectations are so far removed from reality, as in the case of Ron and Mary Lou. But on such experiences the door of love opens or closes. Because the hinge experiences sometimes occur over a long period of time, people are not aware of any single moment of decision. That's why people frequently decide it is a gradual "falling out" of love. It is gradual but it is not falling. It is a gradual process of deciding not to love. Or it is the gradual coming to consciousness of a decision not to love.

Notion Three was that the secret to a loving relationship is finding the person who is right for you.

———————— 💔 ————————

Truth Three: The secret to a loving relationship is two people who work constantly at loving.

———————————————————

There is not *one* person "out there" who is *the* right one for anybody. Our first reaction to this truth ought to be a sense of relief. There are, after all, millions of people "out there."

The really dangerous thing about Notion Three, however, is that it encourages people to misplace or misdirect their focus. If you are looking for Mr. or Ms. Right then you set yourself up to focus on the other and not on yourself. Is this person right for me? Or would so-and-so be more right for me? And so you measure people against one another, comparing their attributes and characteristics.

It is more helpful if people reverse their focus and direct it at themselves. The fact is, I am somewhat different when I am with person A than when I am with person B. I show different aspects of myself or I inhibit different aspects of myself, depending upon the person I am with. By focusing on myself, by consciously considering which "me" I like the best, which "me" is the most authentic, which me is the least "put on," I will have the more important perspective. The question is not so much whether the other person is right for me as it is whether or not *I* am right for me when I am with that person. "Am I the right person for me when I am with you?" That's the question which needs to be answered.

The real truth about what makes for a loving relationship is that it takes two people who work constantly at loving. And that's not much of a secret. Or it shouldn't be.

The first key word in that truth is the word *work.* Loving is work. It is hard work. It is also enjoyable work. It is work that can be fun. But it is work. It requires the expenditure of energy. It requires an investment of time. It requires a number of different behaviors. Real loving is not an attitude or a feeling or an expression in words. Real loving is work.

The second key word is *loving.* That's what one has to work at. This part of the truth is new in the American consciousness regarding the intimate component of a marriage. In the past the focus was very much on *roles,* not on loving. Men had their role and women had theirs. Men were supposed to be breadwinners and provide the financial stability for the marriage. Women were supposed to be mothers and homemakers. Men did the thinking. Women did the feeling.

What made relationships work was both men and women fulfilling the demands of their social role. That's why I hear a man defend himself from the accusation that he does not love his wife by telling me that he goes to work every day to support her, or that he provides for her and that is how he wants the world to know he is demonstrating his love. He is perplexed when I tell him it is possible that he goes to work *because* he loves his wife but that is not really *how* to love. Going to work is not doing the work of loving. In the next chapter I will explain what I believe the work of loving is.

The third key word is *constantly.* I have been listening to the narratives people tell of their relationships for a long time. I can't say how many I've heard, but it's at least a couple thousand. And I've never heard one story about a relationship that never was loving at all.

The time when virtually every relationship can be counted on to be loving is during the courtship and extending into the marriage for at least several months. But for so many couples, by the end of the third year or shortly after the birth of the first child the quality of love and intimacy in the relationship has slipped considerably. It was that phenomenon that caused many people in the 1960s and '70s to decide that the wedding was the culprit. Weddings were what ruined relationships. So people began just living together so that marriage wouldn't spoil the relationship. It didn't work. The wedding wasn't the culprit. And it isn't marriage that destroys intimacy. But I can see why people thought so. You see, the wedding triggers a shift in the priorities of people. Up to the wedding, the role that each gives high priority to is that of *lover.* Each may do other things. Each may have a job, friends, families, and other interests, but each gives the highest priority to being *lover.*

The shift that occurs, either after the wedding or certainly after the birth of the first child, is that men move their breadwinner and provider role to a higher priority, and women give higher priority to their mother and homemaker roles. Over time the role of *lover* sinks lower and lower on each one's priority ladder. And, like any skills that go unused, the lover skills eventually just atrophy. Now the man's best investment of his time, his energy, and his focus are put into his work. And the woman's go into the children, the home, and sometimes her career, too.

"Charlie used to be so thoughtful and caring," Amy said. *"He used to pick me up every day and take me to work; he would call at least once a day to see how my day was going; and he would pick me up and take me home."* That's the way it used to be. Amy is dismayed because *"today my car wouldn't start and I called Charlie, who was already at work, to see if he could give me a ride, and he said he was too busy and I should just take a cab."*

Or consider the case of Don. *"I'm ashamed to admit I'm jealous of my own children. I watch the way Kay lavishes attention and affection on them, the way she hugs and kisses them at bedtime. I don't get that kind of quality affection from her anymore. In fact, it seems like she wears herself out on the kids and there's nothing left for me."*

What I am obviously suggesting is that to maintain a high-quality intimate and loving relationship requires that each continue to give considerable priority to the lover role. Couples must be determined not to let those skills atrophy.

No one expects that twenty years into a relationship partners will be lovers in exactly the way they were in the first six months. The initial intensity and excitement will not be maintained in even the best of marriages. But two people twenty, thirty, or fifty years into a relationship can still give priority to the role of lover. They had better, at any rate, because that's the secret to a loving relationship that endures—two people who work constantly at loving.

Everyone in the shoe store got a kick out of Marvin and Leona. They were in their seventies and had been married for fifty-two years, but they acted like newlyweds. They kidded each other. It was obvious that they enjoyed being with each other and managed to find some delight in something as mundane as buying a pair of shoes. More than one sales clerk could only wish to be as happy after fifty or more years of marriage. Marvin and Leona were still working at loving and still enjoying it.

Notion Four was that the key to Mr. or Ms. Right is sexual compatibility.

Truth Four: You can be sexually compatible with a million persons.
(Obviously a somewhat dangerous truth.)

The truth is that sex is not the "key" to love. Don't misunderstand. I am not even remotely suggesting that sex is a trivial component in a loving relationship. Sex is never trivial. Lots of people have talked about something called "recreational sex," and by that term suggest that two people can play sex together as casually as they might play tennis together. Just for the fun of it. Of course sex should be fun. Sex belongs to the "playful" part of humanness. In other words, in addition to being *Homo sapiens* (the being who thinks) and *Homo habilis* (the being who fabricates) people are also *Homo ludens* (the being who plays). But when we play sexually we play with more than a part of ourselves, our sexual organs. The whole person is involved, for better or for worse. That is why if some part of our personhood is not working well our sex play will be affected. And it is why whole persons can be hurt by sex play.

Put another way, sex, like any kind of play, has its own rules. If you are going to play tennis then you have to play by tennis rules, not by the rules of volleyball. Sex play requires a level of commitment or the play just doesn't work very well. That's because quality sex play involves the capacity to abandon oneself entirely to the play. That in turn requires a measure of trust. That is why "casual sex" is really an oxymoron.

So the first important rule about sex is that, over time, trust in and commitment to one another must be present or our body's sexual function just won't respond very well.

Another important rule about sex is that sexual enjoyment is mutual. That means that one person's pleasure enhances the other's pleasure. Sex is not two people playing solos. It is two people playing in harmony with each other, each one contributing to the beauty (and pleasure) of the other. When only one is pleasured most of the time, sex will quickly become dysfunctional.

Yet another rule about sex is that it helps to be creative, spontaneous, and inventive. Couples should avoid getting into "ruts" of certain times, certain places, or certain routines. Special candlelight dinners, special weekend trips, and little surprises add vitality to the sexual life of a couple.

But my real point is that love is the key to great sex, not the other way around. I have seen a number of couples through the years who were not having great sex. Anything but. Their relationships were troubled by moderate to severe sexual dysfunction. But the partners in each couple were committed and devoted to each other enough to work on the causes of their dysfunction. Their commitment to love each other gave them the courage to do whatever exercises or therapy they needed to do in order to raise the quality of their sex play.

I would agree to use the term "recreational sex" if by it people meant the consequence of quality sex play, namely that people are renewed, re-created, and reborn as persons.

The danger of the cultural falsehood is that people are encouraged to think that "great sex means great love." Or that if you have a very erotic and exciting sexual encounter with someone you have found Mr. or Ms. Right. Lots of people who have experienced a dramatic deterioration in the sexual component of their relationship can get to the point that they cannot stand to be touched any more by that someone who used to be very exciting. So sex is not the key to love. The truth is that love is the key to sex. That is, the quality of the sexual relationship will be determined by the quality of loving experienced in the total relationship.

Notion Five was that loving is something everybody knows how to do.

Truth Five: Loving is something everybody has to learn how to do.

The truth is we must learn how to love. It is not some natural capacity that we are born with. I do believe that we are born with the potential to love. Human beings all have a great need for connectedness. I agree with William Glasser, who teaches that we have a "genetic instruction" to be connected to others.[1] But we have to learn (by trial and error) how to make and how to sustain connectedness with others in ways that give us a sense of happiness and well being. We have the need, desire, or "genetic instruction," but we have to learn the strategies. The strategies are not just there. The strategies do not "come naturally."

So what's the problem? Why aren't we learning strategies? The answer is complex. We are learning some strategies—in the marriages we grow up in, the marriages of our parents. But that's a "good news-bad

1. Glasser, *Control Theory*

news" situation. It's good news if our parents had good relationships. Then we saw some good strategies (open communication, displays of affection, etc.). But in many more cases what we saw were not good strategies. That's what I hear in my practice. I talk to people who never saw their parents display affection; never saw them do problem solving; never saw them communicate meaningfully. But they saw them fight; saw them manipulate each other; saw them employ distancing strategies; saw them even be viciously abusive.

Tom grew up in a home in which he saw and heard his parents have some conflicts. They faced them openly. They discussed their different points of view and each listened to the other. So Tom was not thrown for a loop when he and Angie got into a conflict about their vacation plans. He encouraged her point of view and he listened to it. He then stated his own, and they were able to pinpoint their differences and arrive at a solution.

Vanessa, on the other hand, grew up in a family invaded by alcohol. She saw her parents fight from Friday night to Sunday night. They hurled the most obscene insults at each other. Nineteen years into her own marriage she is engaged in the same behavior.

Bob and Shirley have two sets of twins and five children under the age of six. Shirley is exhausted, depressed, and angry because she is getting no help at all from Bob. She wonders if there is something wrong with her that she can't keep up with it all. (There isn't.) Bob doesn't see what is "such a big deal," and he insists he is tired after a hectic day at the office. Bob never saw his own father model any helping behavior in the home. He has no pictures in his head of father vacuuming, doing dishes, or bathing children, so he doesn't "see" what he could be doing. If Shirley will ask him for some specific behaviors, Bob can overcome a bad strategy he learned in his family of origin.

But there's more to this question of learning strategies. It has to do with how our expectations regarding marriage and loving relationships have changed (Chapter 1). Being a good wife or husband meant something different fifty years ago than it does today. Being a good husband or wife *used* to mean how you performed the *role* expected of you in society much more than anything else. Being a good husband meant primarily being a good provider. Being a good wife meant primarily being a good "emotional center" of the home and family. Today being a good husband or wife means much more. It means learning how to be a responsible partner in producing a high quality of intimacy. It is not so much a matter of learning how to be good at some social role as it is learning how to be a good lover.

I was deeply moved many years ago by reading Erich Fromm's book *The Art of Loving*.[2] I like that notion—that loving is an art. And it is in that sense that I talk about learning how to do loving. Playing a musical instrument is an art; loving is an art. That is to say, one can just take a few lessons to do it well enough to get by. Or one can continue to practice and

---

2. Erich Fromm, *The Art of Loving* (New York: Harper and Row, 1956)

learn almost all through life. Learning to love is like that. It is something that we can get better at all the time, as all through life we learn new strategies and practice faithfully.

Chapter 4

♥

How to Do Loving

For some years now I've had a problem with the word "love." I have a problem for two reasons. First, because the word, as a noun, is singular. I am not a linguist but I believe that when we use singular nouns we intellectually conceptualize *one* thing or phenomenon: Love is one thing.

I'm not arguing here about definitions as such, but about the way we conceptualize love as a singular noun. "Please love me," someone pleads. And because we think of love as one thing, the person to whom that plea is directed thinks of one kind of thing to do.

My second reason for having a problem with the word "love" is that it is an abstract noun. That's another good news-bad news story. Good news because it gives poets, songwriters, playwrights, and psychologists plenty of freedom to be creative and imaginative. But the bad news is that even the most poetic and beautiful expressions of love seldom are helpful, either for the person who pleads to be loved or for the person to whom that plea is directed.

We have all these songs that sing of what love is like but they do not offer much concrete help. Example: "Love is like a river." Just how helpful is that notion to someone who has just been asked, "Please love me." How precisely does one love like a river?

I'm not putting down that song or any other that sings of love's various aspects. Even love poetry has the same problem. "How do I love thee? Let me count the ways."[1] A classic of romantic poetry. But, truth is,

---

1. Elizabeth Barrett Browning, *Sonnets from the Portuguese*

not much help to the person feeling quite unloved or the person who desires very much to help someone else feel loved.

I do not want to get into an argument about definitions. But I do want to assert that at some point "love" must be something more than feeling, something more than all the beautiful metaphors and similes of poets and songwriters. At some point love must be translated into concrete activity. Love may involve some feelings but it *must* also involve some behavior.

I prefer to use the term "loving" instead of "love" whenever possible. "Loving" is the present active participle of the verb "to love." I like it because it is "present" and it's "active." Loving, in other words, is not saying to someone, "I love you." It is doing the actions of loving.

Lots of people have some very sincere intentions behind the expression "I love you." I suspect that the more truthful expression would really be, "I want to love you."

I define love as the personal investment of one person toward another, which fills a unique set of needs for that other. Loving involves both an intention (want to) and the expression of that intention in concrete behaviors which fill certain needs for people.

As a matter of fact, I believe that there are five such needs. Not one need, but five different needs. I didn't really discover these five needs. I learned about them by listening to people as they talked about not feeling loved. When one or more of these needs goes unfilled for some time, people feel unloved.

I believe that we are born with these needs and that they are with us until we die. These five needs are just as involved in the action of loving children as they are in loving lovers and spouses. Or grandparents, for that matter.

The five needs are attention, recognition, respect, affection, and separateness.

Attention

We need people to talk to us. People to answer our questions. People to direct questions at us. People to engage us in real dialogue. We want to feel that when we are talking to people they want to be talking to us and have really connected to us. We respond to the genuine interest others have in us. And we feel it when that interest is not there, when we are being tolerated instead of connected by *attention.*

All of us have seen our children act up if they experience being ignored too much. Parents are advised to notice their children's good behavior so that children won't learn to gain attention by misbehaving. Most of us have experienced the disappointment of having someone important to us not notice our new clothes or new hairstyle. And all of us have experienced the anger and frustration of not being listened to.

My experience, in fact, has been that lack of attention or low-quality attention is the most frequent complaint of women about their lovers or spouses. When I ask a woman what is wrong with her relationship, most often her answer has to do with the lack of attention.

Fran was very upset about a pattern she noticed in her marriage. It was that Carl never seemed able to give her his undivided attention. She saw that his real focus seemed to be watching TV, reading a magazine, or anything else. Carl insisted he could do two things at once, but Fran still felt slighted. She was also aware that almost any time she suggested that they go out to dinner or to a movie, Carl always suggested that they call another couple to go along. It was as though he didn't ever want to be with her alone. "I just never feel special to him," she said.

The same phenomenon can be seen from another direction. Some of my female clients are involved with someone outside the marriage or primary relationship. And when we examine the dynamics of that relationship we usually discover that the increased or better-quality attention is what drew the woman to that person, and keeps her there.

I am definitely not saying that my male clients do not need attention. Nor am I saying that men never complain about non-attention from female lovers or wives. But such men are definitely in the minority. I think they are in the minority for two reasons.

First, because they don't have much to complain about in that respect. They get a lot of attention from wives and lovers. Women listen well to men. They focus on them. They cater to them. That's the traditional pattern in America.

Second, I believe men take a lot of their attention needs to the *work arena* rather than the *intimacy arena* of life. At any rate, I have concluded that women tend to assess the quality of any relationship they are in on the basis of the quality of attention they get.

Recognition

Recognition goes beyond attention. It is what your child expects when coming home from school with an excellent paper or performing some feat of athletic skill. That child can read your pride in your eyes. That's recognition. It is the momentary or extended experience of being special in the eyes of a significant other. What you want to experience in an adult loving relationship is that your lover or spouse is proud of what you are or what you accomplish.

This second need is the most frequent area of complaint of my male clients. Because of the way men are socialized in America they want to experience that their lovers or spouses see them as "heroes." That's why men can be so devastated by criticism from a woman. That's also why they do so much "macho" posturing from about age twelve on up. A popular American country western song sang of "starting out to be hero and ending up a zero can scar a man deep in his soul."[2] And it's true. I've seen many a man

2. Larry Gatlin and the Gatlin Brothers, "All the Gold in California," 1979

rendered sexually dysfunctional by "becoming a zero" to his lover.

But just as the need for attention is not limited to women, the need for recognition is not limited to just men. Women have it too. It's just that women don't complain as often about men not being proud of them. In any case, I think that men assess the quality of their relationships mostly on the basis of recognition.

This is also confirmed by the dynamics of the affairs men get involved in. As a man answered, when I asked him why he took the risks involved in an affair, "It's simple. She makes me feel ten feet tall. My wife makes me feel like a loser." That's recognition.

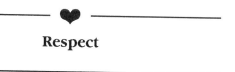

Respect

Much is written today about self-esteem. There are workshops and seminars on how to raise your self-esteem. There are support groups for people who are working together on improving their self-esteem. It is a movement whose time has come. I've taught all-day workshops on self-esteem, and offer techniques to parents on how to parent so that children grow up with healthy self-esteem. I define self-esteem as the value or worth which you confer on yourself.

Self-esteem is related to our *respect* need but the two are not the same. The difference is that *respect* is the value or worth *others confer on us* in the way they treat us. Self-esteem is self-conferred. Respect is other conferred. Self-esteem and respect are mutually related. That is, it is difficult to maintain self-esteem when significant others are treating us abusively. But it is also true that people with poor self-esteem tolerate abusive persons in their lives.

Loving involves the conferring of value and worth on the beloved, filling the human need for respect. This is accomplished in a number of ways. In the first place, it involves respect for the body, the personhood, and the personality of one's beloved. It means that bodies are not hit or pushed, personhoods are not ignored, and personalities are not attacked or criticized. Respect is experienced by someone as being an equal partner in the relationship. It means experiencing consideration for one's feelings. It means experiencing that one's ideas, one's tastes, one's likes and dislikes, one's time, and talents count equal to those of one's partner. Not more or less than, but equal to.

"Something is wrong with my marriage," she says, "and I can't figure out what it is. But I'll tell you what happened. Last month my husband said, 'I want to see this movie, let's go Saturday.' So I went to the movie. But last week when I told him I wanted to see a certain movie he said 'I don't want to see that movie, go with your sister.'"

What's wrong with that relationship is that when he wants to do something it's important enough that she should do it with him, but when she wants to do something it may not be important enough for him to do it with her. That kind of inequality does not confer value or respect. It does the opposite.

—————————— ♥ ——————————

Affection

Everyone knows about this need. It is the broad concept of human contact which includes but is not narrowly limited to sexual relations.

Human beings have a fundamental need to be hugged, to be touched appropriately and lovingly by others. In loving relationships we expect to be kissed, caressed, and fondled. I am always amazed, in fact, at how awkward so many people feel about doing touching or being touched, even persons who have not been victimized by abusive touching or contact. I continue to stress to people that the brain is the most important sex organ but the skin which covers our bodies is our largest sex organ. We simply need to take more time to learn how to touch one another more.

Such was the case with Sandy and Craig. Both wanted affection, but each experienced a problem with the other. Craig complained that when he approached Sandy she "always found something wrong" with the way he touched her. He thought she was somewhat frigid. Sandy denied the frigidity claim and insisted she was afraid to tell Craig what the problem was for fear she would hurt his feelings. The problem was that he was too sudden and too rough. He also seemed to concentrate only on the genital area. She wanted to be held and to have her back caressed, too, but didn't know how to ask for that. Counseling taught them how to talk about it, and after getting some explanation on how to do body caressing, their sex life improved considerably.

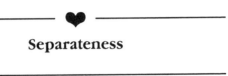

Separateness

Perhaps it sounds strange to talk about a need for separateness as a part of loving. But it's true. We are, after all, separate persons. Two people in a relationship have their own unique histories, personalities, dreams, fantasies, expectations, and individualities. Loving someone means allowing the beloved to be his or her own person, to pursue his or her own path to personal growth and happiness.

But isn't *togetherness* the thing these days? Yes, of course it is, but the best kind of togetherness is the kind created by two whole separate persons. I've often wanted to create a poster which would say

YOU CAN'T MAKE IT WITH SOMEONE ELSE
UNTIL YOU CAN MAKE IT BY YOURSELF!

People who have not developed as individuals do not do well in relationships. They are too dependent, too needy; as though they constantly and desperately need someone to validate their existence.

There was an old country western song which asked the question, "How does it feel to be someone's *only* reason for living?" I'll tell you how it feels. It feels like you are pulling a five-hundred pound rock around. It feels like you are raising an extra child, not sharing, planning, and working with an adult.

I think of separateness in terms of each person having his or her own life's orbit. A relationship involves two people arranging (a conscious, free, and voluntary process) their orbits so they overlap.

Figure 1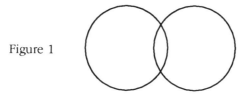

As the illustration shows, each has some place, time, or space alone, and yet they both have some of the same in common. This is a dynamic process which changes on a daily basis, on a seasonal basis, on a work-schedule basis, and even on a life-cycle basis.

Figure 2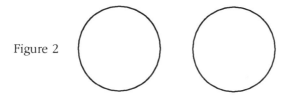

The above arrangement of orbits (figure 2) is obviously not a relationship. There is no overlap at all. These two people may share the same address, but not much more than that.

Figure 3

The orbits in figure 3 indicate another type of relationship, one in which one person lives entirely inside the orbit of another. The person in the smaller orbit (because one always has to diminish oneself in this kind of relationship) must derive virtually all meaning and purpose in life from the dreams and deeds of the other.

Why would anyone ever get into this kind of a relationship? Because there is a payoff for each. The person in the outside orbit gets to control the relationship and so enjoys the power. The person on the inside *apparently* gets security and protection. But it's really an awful alliance or contract these two make. It's a relationship which, in order to survive, demands that neither person grow. Growth on the part of either one will doom the relationship. It is also a tragic relationship because it makes real human loving impossible. Love is only possible in an adult relationship when two people can relate to each other as relatively equal in power.

Note something else about comparing the first pair of orbits to this last pair. In the first pair each person spends some time away from the other, has some experiences apart from the other, and can therefore bring into the common space and time something new, something stimulating. So relationships in which each person has some separateness are potentially more exciting and stimulating, even though they demand more effort.

I find it helpful to imagine that these five needs are like five "buckets" we carry around inside of us— buckets labeled *attention, recognition, respect, affec-*

tion, and *separateness.* They are not always lined up inside us in exactly that order, and they are not all the same size. They are dynamic buckets that move around and shrink or expand in size.

Now I can fill in a little better some of the gaps from my earlier discussion of the notions and truths about loving. In the first place, love does not belong to the mysterious magical realm. Loving is the mutual and reciprocal action of two people who are filling these five needs for each other. You can make a fairly clear and rational assessment of how well you are being loved by assessing the quantity and quality of the attention, recognition, respect, affection, and separateness you are getting. And you can assess the loving you are doing in the same way.

Second, I indicated that loving is something you decide to do. In terms of my "buckets" model, then, when you decide to love someone the first thing you do is extend yourself and invest in that person by filling his or her buckets. The second thing you do is hold your own buckets out for filling. Similarly, when you decide not to love someone (or to stop loving) you do two things also. You stop investing in that person, and you pull your own buckets away from him or her.

That's the reason why you may notice in a relationship gone wrong that nothing you do makes any difference. You may even wonder why, when you try to do that which someone has been asking you to do or has been complaining because you weren't doing it, you are not getting anywhere. In fact, you may experience that what you are doing—just because your lover has wanted you to—now seems not only to fail to please, but actually causes more anger. That's because the person has given up and pulled those buckets away. That person now will not allow you to do loving.

Finally, I indicated that the "secret" to a loving relationship is two people who work constantly at loving. And by "loving" I mean the mutual and reciprocal action of filling each other's buckets— needs for attention, recognition, respect, affection, and separateness. It is not just during the courtship but throughout the years of married living that the work of filling each other's buckets must be done.

Chapter 5

❤

The Tasks of Loving

In the preceding chapter I explained the five needs which have to be filled on a regular basis in order to do loving or in order to be loved by someone. Assuming my five needs are a relevant and meaningful model of how you do loving, I can now turn to examine more closely the "doing" itself.

There are five different aspects to the doing of loving. All of them, however, assume commitment in the first place. By commitment I mean the *will* or determination to love someone followed by action which actualizes that will.

I make that point because my experience is that lots of people do want to love someone. When they say "I love you," they are really saying "I want to love you." The problem is that in many cases wanting to love is not followed by the doing, the action of loving. The will to love must be put into action in order for "buckets" to be filled. Otherwise loving remains just an unfulfilled wish or promise. I may sincerely want to do lots of things—lose weight, become more physically fit, eat better, or learn to play a banjo—but if the wanting is not translated into something I do with my time and energy, then wishing will never make it so.

So commitment to another person or to a relationship means both the will to love and specific behaviors which are energized by that will and which result in needs being filled for another person. Translating *will* into *action* involves five different aspects of loving.

The first aspect of loving is sensitivity.

By sensitivity I mean the ability or capacity to be aware of what the beloved is feeling. I'm not talking about doing mind reading. And most people don't like being told what they are thinking or feeling. The kind of sensitivity I mean is the capacity to empathize with another; to notice that someone is hurting without necessarily knowing why. It is the capacity to "read" another person's signs. "You seem down tonight." "Are you having a headache?" "I can tell you don't like my suggestion very much." "You seemed bothered about something." "You got a haircut today." Those are the kinds of statements or questions which reveal a capacity to be sensitive.

Over a period of time loving, sensitive people should get to know each other well enough to anticipate what will "go over" with the other person and what will not. I am always amazed at how some people can live with each other for many years and still seem not to know that certain behavior offends the other, or that the lack of certain behavior causes a deep hurt.

Sometimes the hurt is caused unintentionally because the loved one's response to someone is taken in a different way than intended.

Frank was laid off from his well-paying job as an electrician, and it came at a time when he was just feeling good about getting his family almost out of debt. He took a much lower-paying job just to keep some income coming in to pay the bills, but he felt guilty about not being a better provider for the family. Being a good provider is something that men in our culture associate with manhood and success. Frank's wife, Karen, knew her husband was hurt about being laid off, and she wanted to encourage him to get a better-paying job even if it meant going longer without work. But every time she mentioned "better job" Frank felt more of a failure. Karen insisted she only wanted him to have a job that would help his self-esteem. If she had been a little more sensitive she might have changed the way she talked about a "better-paying job."

Doing loving requires, then, some degree of sensitivity. In terms of my bucket model it means knowing which bucket is up front at just this particular time and also how large or how empty it is. A couple who attended one of my workshops and learned about the buckets went out almost immediately afterward and purchased red and green sets of buckets. They labeled them appropriately and agreed on a particular place in their home where they would daily display their buckets in the appropriate order of priority. I think that's a good way to begin. I hope that someday they would not need the display if they learn the lessons of sensitivity. Unless someone is deliberately hiding a lot of feelings (which is not unusual in dysfunctional relationships), sensitive people can learn to do a pretty good job of reading each other.

The second aspect of loving is filling the appropriate bucket to an appropriate level.

One must know which bucket is up front and empty. That bucket needs to be filled, not some other bucket. I know that statement sounds so obvious that it may seem ludicrous even to make a special point of it. But it is not as obvious in practice as it sounds.

First, because, as human beings who are governed by some law of least resistance, we are inclined to want to do those things which are easiest for us to do. We look for ways to expend the least amount of energy over the least amount of time. As the song goes "If it don't come easy better let it go."[1]

Second, because we live in a culture that has brainwashed men and women into believing that there are certain gender-specific ways of doing loving. I am talking about the way in which a consumer economy has persuaded us to think that we show our love by buying the beloved something. When it comes to buying "diamonds say it best," one advertisement says.[2] Buying diamonds, flowers, candy, or whatever is the way to show love in American culture. Whitney Houston is closer to the truth when she sings "Didn't we almost have it all, when love was all we had for giving?"[3]

Of course we enjoy the experience of purchasing and giving gifts—to our children or to our beloveds. But gifts, even expensive gifts, will never take the place of attention, recognition, respect, affection, and separateness—the real needs that require filling in

1. Gibson and Kemp, "If It Don't Come Easy," 1988
2. Helzburgh's Diamonds, advertisement in *Cedar Rapids Gazette* (Cedar Rapids, IA, December 1991)
3. Masser and Jennings, "Didn't We Almost Have It All," 1987

order for us to feel loved. Everyone knows down deep that we can be surrounded with expensive gifts and feel desperately lonely or unloved. Even children are frequently wise enough to know when gifts are given instead of loving. Gifts, even diamonds, are ultimately a poor substitute for love.

Mary made an appointment with me because she was depressed. After the initial interview I told her that she did not appear to have any symptoms of clinical depression, and I wondered about her marriage. She began to cry, and we determined that a second appointment, with her husband, was needed. He came with her to the next session. I explained to each of them about the five buckets and then asked both of them to assess which buckets they thought were probably up front most of the time for each other. I should add that this man sincerely wanted to love his wife. He really cared about her and wanted her to know she was special to him. But he was a busy executive whose career periodically demanded he spend a week to ten days at a time in a city hundreds of miles away. Her "depression" always seemed to hit just before he left on one of his trips.

But he was a sensitive man. He knew she would be down. And that bothered him. So he wanted to do something for her so she wouldn't be so "down" while he was gone. What he would do was to have his secretary pick out a lovely card for his wife and into that card he would insert a round trip ticket to San Francisco and a $500 cashier's check. And he would write a note that said "I love you—have a shopping trip on me." Which, of course, she did.

When asked to assess his wife's emptiest bucket this husband correctly identified attention as the empty bucket up front. Then I invited him to take a look at which bucket he was working the most at filling. It was a clear pattern of filling the separateness bucket.

But, as I said, he sincerely wanted to love his wife. So the next time he flew to that distant city he again sent her a card with a plane ticket in it—but this time the ticket was to the same city he would be in. And this time the note said, "I'll be done by Thursday noon so why not fly down Thursday and we'll spend the rest of the week and the weekend together." Now he was filling the right bucket.

So it isn't always so obvious. People have to learn how to be sensitive and how to fill the right bucket. A part of the fun of loving is figuring out new, creative, and imaginative ways of filling buckets for each other.

The third aspect of loving is that we have to risk holding our own buckets out to someone else.

A loving relationship has a necessary mutuality about it. Both partners have to invest themselves in each other and both have to risk holding their buckets out to each other.

Why is that so important? Simply because it does involve a risk. The risk is that someone will say no, that someone will just turn around and walk away instead of filling your buckets. The risk is that in the very act of holding your buckets out you are making yourself vulnerable to rejection. The more vulnerable you make yourself the more you can be hurt.

I often see people who want to know how they can find a loving relationship without risking rejection or abandonment. They've been deeply hurt by one or more previous rejections and just don't think they can go through that awful pain again.

That's the way Angela felt. Her second marriage had ended in a shocking revelation. Her husband, Harry, was still married to another woman. She discovered this just days after her first anniversary. Her first marriage had ended when her husband left her for another woman. Two years after that Angela had met Harry. He was very caring and thoughtful, and he seemed to connect right away with her eight-year-old son, Tony. Then came the revelation. She was hurt beyond description; doubly hurt because Tony felt abandoned again. Angela came to me for counseling and specifically requested to learn how to have a relationship without being vulnerable. "I can't stand to be hurt again, and neither can Tony."

I understand that pain. I really do. But there is no way to find love without risking that pain. Building a thick high wall around yourself to keep from being hurt will only isolate you from people. It will not get you love or protect you from pain. Defensive walls alienate others and make you very, very lonely.

So you will have to risk. You can be sensible about how soon in a relationship to make yourself vulnerable. You can learn to gauge the investing and risking the other person is doing. The absence of that investing or risking by your partner is a major clue that this is not the time to risk all and make yourself vulnerable to that person. I am suggesting that you need to learn how to assess the degree of mutuality in a relationship and then to risk accordingly.

Jill came in for counseling because her third relationship with a young man was faltering. "I keep hearing 'I need more space' or some request like that from the men I get involved with," she said, "and I'm getting tired of it. What's wrong with men?" While admitting that some young men of college age are apparently reluctant to make commitments, I suggested that Jill tell me more details about her relationships with men. When she did so, it was obvious that by the fourth or fifth date in each case, Jill was already thinking marriage and life-long relationship. She was committing for life. When I asked her if she had experienced that same degree of commitment from the men she was dating she admitted that she had not. She also admitted that not-so-deep-down she knew she had been putting more of herself into each relationship than had the man.

This is a problem that very many people have. They invest and invest and seem not to notice that the partner is not investing at anything near the same pace. Or they make themselves quite vulnerable before there is any real evidence that it is appropriate to do so with this particular person. People who have this problem usually come from families of origin with severe to moderate dysfunction, as I will explain later.

---------------------- ❤ ----------------------

The fourth aspect of loving is what I call telling and asking.

This aspect of the task of loving is always important, but particularly in the early stages when we are learning to know and to "read" each other. None of us is equipped with any mind-reading ability that works even most, let alone all, of the time. We usually can seem to do that only when it is quite obvious.

Most of us can remember how easily we talked in the early stage of the relationship—when we were still getting acquainted. There are two reasons why there was so much more communication then. First, because a lot of the conversations were about pretty superficial stuff. We talked about such topics as music, food, movies, friends, and family. It's easier to reveal our thinking about less serious topics. It's a lot more risky to open up and talk about things that reveal our deepest values and beliefs.

Linda and Dick were in counseling doing a "marital review," which begins with talking about the circumstances under which a couple first meets, and what attracted them to each other. Linda specifically recalled that the night they first met they were attending the birthday party of her cousin, and Dick had come with a male friend of his. It turned out Linda and Dick were originally from neighboring small towns. They spent almost all the time at the party talking with each other and, in fact, spent most of the night—till about 4 a.m.—talking. Both mentioned that one of the things that attracted them to each other was that it was so easy to talk together.

Now they had been married for ten years, and they had just spent about an hour driving to this appointment. The entire ride had been in silence. "I don't know what Dick thinks about anything important," she said. "His father just died about three months ago and he has never talked about it. I know he and his dad did not get along the last two years and I think something is bothering him, but he won't open up." Talking about his feelings about his dad's death was very difficult for Dick.

The second reason communication is better early in the relationship is because, in the flush and excitement of a new relationship, we are brave enough to risk more. Later on we learn that what we reveal may be used against us. Or we may feel that we are risking disapproval and negative judgments. Strangely, we may be braver in the early stage of a relationship, enough to risk making ourselves vulnerable to another person, than later on—even though one might think that later, when a loving relationship has had a chance to develop and mature, we would feel braver than at the beginning.

In an intimate moment with Joan, Walter revealed that he had always had a secret ambition to be a minister. This was true in spite of the fact that he had grown up in a home in which no one had ever even attended a church. Several weeks later, they were out with friends and someone told a dirty joke. Joan suggested there should be no more such jokes because they would be surprised to know Walter had a secret urge to be a minister. Walter said nothing when everybody laughed, but the look on his face made it clear to Joan that she had touched a nerve in Walter that would have been better left untouched.

Another reason people frequently give for not talking about what they think or feel is that they do not want to upset the lover or spouse. And it is true that your spouse or lover may indeed get upset. But I have noticed that, with few exceptions, whatever unhappiness you are trying to prevent by remaining quiet usually develops anyway as a result of the silence or failure to communicate.

John's financial assistance to his son by a previous marriage was a constant source of tension between him and Sue. He arranged with his son not to call his home anymore, especially when the son was going to ask for money. John insisted he made this arrangement to prevent Sue from getting upset. But Sue usually managed to find out anyway, and was upset as much by the steps John took to hide his behavior as by the behavior itself.

In a healthy loving relationship it is appropriate to talk about what you are thinking and feeling. In a healthy loving relationship it is not necessary to "protect" your lover or spouse from what you are thinking or feeling. My experience, in fact, is that "protectors" always turn out to be "persecutors." Which is to say that the "protected" one over time feels a lot more persecuted by what you do to protect him or her than if you just revealed the truth. I think the truth is that most of the time when we are being "protectors" of others we are really protecting only ourselves.

It is also appropriate in a healthy relationship to ask for what you want or need. It is not realistic to think that your lover or spouse will always anticipate what your wants or needs are. I use an exercise with my clients to teach and encourage both asking and offering in their relationships. I take a blank piece of paper and at the top of one side I start the sentence, "Three things I wish you would do for me next week are:" At the top of the other side I write, "Three things I would like to do for you are:" There are only two rules for this exercise. Rule One: You cannot ask for something you know your lover or spouse does not like to do (for whatever reason). Rule Two: You must fill in the blanks with behaviors that could be filmed or recorded. That is, they must be specific, objective behaviors. For example: "Give me a ten-minute back rub on Wednesday night." (Not, "Help me relax more.")

Remember, loving as a process of mutual bucket filling is really a continuous flow of specific behaviors. And in good relationships we have the responsibility both to offer what we have to give and to ask for what we want or need. Couples who can do this seldom complain of communication problems.

The fifth aspect of loving has to do with a task people must do for themselves—the task of "bucket fixing" or "bucket repair."

We just don't make it to the adult stage of our life cycle without having developed some "holes" in our buckets. In some cases the whole bottom is out of the bucket. The problem is immediately obvious. How do you fill a bucket with holes in it or with the bottom completely gone? You can't fill a bucket in that condition.

Where do the holes come from? They come from our childhood experiences. They come from the experiences we have had with our earliest caretakers, usually our parents. Our parents or parent surrogates were the first persons we depended on to fill our buckets. When they did not do a perfect job of filling them or when they maliciously neglected them, we developed small to gaping holes in our buckets.

For example, a man has grown up in a family in which he never seemed to experience mother's approval. No matter what he accomplished, she never could verbalize that she was proud of him. He also has no conscious memory of ever being hugged by his mother. He has grown up to be a man with holes in his recognition and affection buckets. What is even more astounding is that he will probably be attracted to women who are somewhat withholding of both affection and recognition. As Harville Hendrix has so adequately described in *Getting The Love You Want*,[4] it is as though we need to find a lover or spouse with whom we can reset the stage of our childhood lives emotionally, and give the stories happy endings instead of the unhappy endings of our childhoods. But

---

4. Hendrix, *Getting the Love You Want*

they usually turn out to have the same endings—our buckets still feel quite empty. Even when someone does try to fill our buckets it won't work if the buckets have gaping holes in them. And, as you can imagine, in most relationships both partners have such buckets.

This is why I spend a good deal of time with all my clients doing family-of-origin workups. And this is why parents are often asked to get involved with their adult children, to heal old wounds—or more correctly to fix some of the broken buckets from childhood.

How do we go about fixing our buckets? By first understanding something about the emotional dynamics of our relationships with our parents or first caretakers. Then by dealing with those emotional issues—with the actual people whenever possible. Many of us have never talked with our parents about some of those childhood issues. Some of us even deny that we have any problems related to childhood. Some go too far and want to blame everything on parents. But I have often seen the beneficial results for our own adult relationships which come from dealing with our parents about childhood issues.

Wanda complained that husband Tom did not really listen to her point of view. She believed that quite often her ideas, feelings, and priorities did not get fair and equal consideration with his.

Tom indicated that he had often heard Wanda make that complaint. He admitted that sometimes he probably had been insensitive to her feelings, and there had been instances when he put his priorities ahead of hers. But he didn't think that happened as often as Wanda complained that it did.

During the family-of-origin workup Wanda talked about her relationship with her father, from when she was age five to twelve. She had many vivid and painful memories from that period of her childhood. She expressed the opinion that her father had often been unfair in his punishment. The innocent ones were often punished with the guilty. She also could remember being told regularly that her father was not interested in hearing her point of view. When she sometimes had expressed an opinion it had not been acknowledged by her father (creating an experience called invalidation).

Because of the similarity between the complaints Wanda had about her father and Tom, I suggested that she work on some of the unresolved issues with her father in a session with her father present. Wanda agreed and her father agreed to come. Wanda was very nervous at the beginning of that session. But she managed to pour out her frustration and pain to her father.

Father handled the confrontation well and did not become defensive. He acknowledged his arbitrary and invalidating parenting style. He apologized to Wanda and she accepted. They embraced with tears all around. It was a poignant scene.

In later sessions Tom and Wanda both agreed that the session with Wanda's father had been the turning point both in the therapy and in their marriage.

This can be done even when parents are deceased or, because of poor health, unable to participate, but it does take much longer. I have suggested in this case that a person write a letter to the parent and get the hurt and pain out in the open. I forbid the client to do any self-censoring. Let the raw pain, hurt, anger be bared. This letter may or may not be mailed. Then I ask my client to write the letter he or she would like to get from the parent in response. I have found this to be a helpful and healing process.

Another answer to the question of how you fix your own buckets is: Work on self-esteem. That is because self-esteem involves a healthy form of self-love, a way by which you learn to, partly at least, fill your own buckets. When you are creating self-esteem you are usually giving yourself attention, recognition, and respect, and you are usually learning to value your own uniqueness and individuality.

One final observation about the task of bucket fixing: You must fix your own buckets. Nobody can fix your buckets for you. The most loving and caring of lovers or spouses cannot do it for you. And you cannot fix anyone else's broken buckets either. You can only fix your own. There are those who see people with broken buckets and are quite attracted to them. Often both are from somewhat dysfunctional families. They imagine that they will fix each other. Sadly and pathetically, it won't work. Bucket fixing is something you must accomplish individually. A therapist can help facilitate that process for you, but it still must be a lonely process of growth. Fortunately, at any stage of life it is possible to fix your own bucket so that you can richly give and receive love.[5]

---

5. What I call "bucket fixing" John Bradshaw calls "healing your inner child." See *Homecoming* (New York: Bantam, 1990)

Chapter 6

❤

The Nature of Intimacy

In 1990 Augustus Napier and his wife wrote a book titled *The Fragile Bond*.[1] It was the subtitle that caught my eye, however. "How to have a marriage that is enduring, intimate and equal." Those three terms express, I believe, the key values about marriage for the 1990s. We want marriages that endure; we want them to be equal; and we want them to be intimate.

Of these three values, however, only the first is really traditional. So traditional that, in fact, there are people today who believe that since we are living in a culture which practices serial monogamy (one spouse at a time but more than one over a lifetime) even this traditional value is on the way to being discarded. These people claim that marriages which endure till "death do us part" were only possible in a world in which life expectancy was under forty years. Such people insist that just as modern people can look forward to multiple careers, so we are moving to a world in which multiple marriages will be the rule rather than the exception. Certainly current statistics give support to that view. Remarriage is occurring at the rate of 1,300 per day in America and in the year 1990, for the first time ever, just over half the weddings were remarriages rather than first marriages.[2]

Nevertheless, I believe that human beings are among the pair bonded of the earth's species. And I believe the best interests of children are served by

1. Augustus Napier, *The Fragile Bond* (New York: Harper and Row, 1988)
2. Mark Bruce Rosin, *Stepfathering* (New York: Simon and Schuster, 1987) 12.

growing up in families that are stable and loving. So count me among those who believe that *enduring* is a value we will continue to place on marriage. But I also believe that endurance will *not* be the core value, that most crucial value which must be at least partially fulfilled in order for a marriage to be considered endurable.

Back in about 1959, I was privileged to get some of my first lessons about marital counseling from David Mace.[3] In a seminar which I attended David told a group of us that when you want to discover what values a culture attaches to marriage, you can discover the answer by looking at the culture's divorce laws. As divorce laws change you can get a picture of the changing values of a culture.

Using Mace's insight, what do the changing divorce laws of our culture reveal about the changing of values in regard to love and marriage? One does not need legal credentials to observe that, as a culture, we have moved from adversarial divorce to "no fault" divorce. That is, we have moved from a position in which a "plaintiff" had to charge a "defendant" with some kind of "civil crime" and to prove the truth of the charge in a court of law, to a new position in which one does not have to charge a spouse with anything. One merely has to affirm that the legitimate objectives of marriage in the experiences of the "petitioner" are not being met. And even if the other spouse, who

---

3. David Mace is a marriage and family counselor, now retired. He and his wife, Vera, were instrumental in initiating the marriage enrichment movement. He is the author of *We Can Have Better Marriages* (Nashville, TN: Abingdon, 1974).

becomes a "respondent" in no-fault divorce, wants to continue the marriage the dissolution is virtually always granted.

This change in the divorce law from adversarial to no-fault reflects our culture's emphasis on the voluntary freedom we have to make the commitment to marry and the equally voluntary right to withdraw that commitment when what we value about marriage is not being fulfilled. One might say that such a concept of marriage and divorce was predictable in a country which emphasizes personal freedom and the right to the (individual) pursuit of life, liberty, and happiness.

But as much as we value individual freedom, that does not seem to be the core value now associated with marriage. The core value is what we treasure the most, what we look for the most in a relationship. It is the core value on which we base our most critical judgments about marriage. It is in fact the supreme value on which the decisions are made to maintain or to leave a marriage.

Perhaps we can identify the new core value more clearly if we can look at what the previous core value was. My contention is that for centuries the core value associated with marriage was the biological continuity of the family as experienced in the birth of children.

Go back to the Middle Ages, when the power of the Church was exercised all over Europe, and one piece of that power was control over divorce and annulment. Even then, with all the resistance to divorce, there was a way to get it accomplished *if* family continuity was threatened by the lack of an heir. Biological continuity was, I believe, the core value associated with marriage.

In more modern times the evidence for biological continuity was still quite visible as a core value. One can find it in the fact that in many older state statutes in this country infertility was a grounds for divorce, in fact it was usually found to be one of the first three grounds.

Further evidence for biological continuity of the family as a core value of marriage can be seen in the fact that until the first quarter of this century husbands routinely got custody of children in the event of divorce. Granted that this was probably derived from much earlier times when children were considered the "property" of the father. But it lasted into this century in this country because biological continuity was most obvious in the continuity of the father's family name.

The final bit of evidence I offer as proof of biological continuity as the traditional core value is the long-standing pattern of husbands and wives who continued to stay in dysfunctional marriages for the sake of the children. Many of these left those marriages once children were raised, which accounts for a clustering of divorces after around twenty years of marriage.

I am not suggesting that biological continuity—having children—is no longer a value of marriage. It is, and it is a highly significant value. But it is not the core value any more. That makes it so different from our grandparents' world. Maybe that's why family reunions were so important to them—those reunions provided the opportunities for the biological continuity to become visible. Even the physical resemblances were a part of that. One could see in the same body shapes, in the same dimples, in the same hair, even in the same bags under the eyes, the continuity of the family.

But that was a different world. Maybe divorces have made family reunions impractical—or maybe too painful. Now the discontinuity is what shows. Suddenly there are stepchildren, and family resemblance is hard to find.

So what is the new core value? I believe it is intimacy. Intimacy is not a new value. Ancient poetry testifies to the presence of intimacy from the very beginnings of recorded history. The heart-to-heart, body-to-body closeness of human intimacy is by no means a modern invention. Long before the Middle Ages and the troubadours, love was in full swing. I think of the frankly erotic poetry in the biblical Song of Solomon. Some anonymous poet, perhaps a rejected lover, knew that "many waters cannot quench the fire of love."[4]

What is new about intimacy, then, is not that it is *a* value but that it has become the *core* value associated with marital love. In fact, when we now think of marital love we think of quality intimacy as its very character.

So what exactly is intimacy? Like love, intimacy is more than one thing. Intimacy has a number of components which blend together. All are necessary for true intimacy. Of course each one of the compo-

---

4. The Song of Solomon 8:6

nents may be present to varying degrees in any relationship. And the degree to which these components are present may vary from time to time. Any one of these components may be developed to a higher degree by persons wanting to develop the total intimacy in their relationship.

Intimacy is first of all physical closeness.

It is sharing the same space and time together. There is a special kind of closeness that develops among people who day after day work in the same office, the same hospital wing, or the same car wash. I know of lots of affairs which began quite innocently, even unintentionally, as two people just started spending lunch break together, or worked next to each other day after day on the production line. Not all intimacy is an affair, however. Two police officers sharing the same squad car for months often become intimate friends. My point is simply that physical proximity over time provides the environment for intimacy to develop. And when people within the same physical proximity also share the same activity, it is even more likely.

Ron and Irene met each other on the assembly line. They were frequently side by side on the same inspection line. They started out just talking about routine topics while on break. Over a period of several months, they wound up eating lunch at the same table in the break room. Like most people, they both had some conflicts in their respective marriages. Neither

*Ron nor Irene was looking for an affair. But each
found the other easy to talk to, and as the weeks passed
by they discovered they had a lot of viewpoints that
were the same. In fact, it was refreshing to discover
support for their individual views because they both
had conflicts with their spouses about some of these
issues.*

*Their friendship just slowly developed over an
eight-month period. Then one day they met for conver-
sation over a drink. It was soon an affair.*

Conversely, it is also true that when two people,
say a married couple, do *not* share time, space, and
activities, it is likely that a certain deterioration in
intimacy will occur. Many couples go from the courtship period, in which they do nearly everything
together, to married life when, some years later, they
do almost nothing together. He has his friends, she has
hers. But they have few together. He has his activities,
she has hers. But they have few activities which they
engage in together. A few couples even take separate
vacations. That is not a recipe for great intimacy.

That is not to say that a couple must do everything
together. Remember that separateness bucket! Either
he or she may have a major activity the other does not
share without doing any damage to intimacy. I am
talking about balance. The question is always one of
how much and how important, and ultimately, of
whether they have enough activities which they share
and enjoy together.

I realize that much of our modern lifestyle can
make physical closeness a bit of a challenge. For one
thing, there is the phenomenon of work shifts that do

not coincide—he works 7 a.m. to 5 p.m. and she works 3 p.m. to midnight. While I realize that sometimes people have little or no control over their hours, I consistently urge couples to do all within their power to adjust their shifts to each other. This is especially true for couples in the first five years of marriage. I believe that irreparable damage can be done to young marriages when daily physical closeness is extremely limited or just impossible.

The situation is even worse for some couples. There are the "commuter marriages" in which one or both spouses leave home early in the morning and return late at night. There are couples who are regularly separated for days at a time over great distances, from traveling sales people to over-the-road truck drivers. Look at the divorce rates for these people and you will see some of the evidence as to the importance of physical closeness. Shared physical space, shared time, and shared activities are essential to quality intimacy.

Intimacy also requires openness.

While physical closeness seems to create some breadth to a relationship an opposite component—openness—creates the depth. Openness has to do with how much of your private inner self you let someone see. It is as though you have a hundred windows behind which there is the bulk of what makes you uniquely who you are—your private thoughts, your feelings, your wishes, your fantasies, your fears, and above all, your secrets. Imagine that shades are pulled down in front of all one hundred windows. The degree of openness you have with anyone is gauged by how many of the shades are raised to show who you really are.

The most exciting, exhilarating stage in a relationship is when two people move beyond the superficial acquaintance stage and into the openness stage. There is something about knowing and becoming known that is intensely exhilarating. That's when couples are amazed at how the time has gone by so quickly, and why some can talk all night and not even feel tired. Knowing and being known is perhaps one of the surest ways of feeling vitally alive. It is proof that we are created for connectedness with others.

But it is also risky. When I open myself up to another I can experience the exhilaration of being known but also the profound sense of vulnerability. A number of years ago John Powell wrote a popular little book called *Why Am I Afraid to Tell You Who I Am?*[5] And the answer was, "I am afraid to tell you who I am because then you might not like me." That is what makes openness risky. You might laugh at my fantasies. You might assess my thoughts to be stupid. You might think my private sexual fantasies are perverted. You might judge me and condemn me. (In fact I might even do that to myself, so I may not even be open with me!)

Ken and Joan were having an intimate dinner to celebrate their seventh wedding anniversary. They

5. John Powell, S.J., *Why Am I Afraid to Tell You Who I Am?* (Allen, TX: Tabor Publishing, a division of DLM, Inc., 1969)

had just been through a rough three months. Ken had been gone a lot and Joan had felt neglected and lonely, as had also been the case in the third year of their marriage. Ken was now going to be off the road and home every night. They had talked with a marriage counselor about renewing their marriage. Both of them had decided that an area in which they needed to improve was opening up and being completely honest with each other.

Joan decided to tell Ken that during the third year of their marriage she had been very lonely and vulnerable. She had taken a class in home decorating just to prevent boredom. She had met a man there and for a two-week period had a relationship with him. She quickly discovered that she did not want to carry on a relationship with him, so she ended it. Now, at this dinner, she just wanted Ken to know so there would be no ghosts between them.

Ken was very quiet for a moment. He then reached up and pinched out both candles and left the table. Three days later he filed for a divorce.

And there is still another level of risk. When you truly open yourself to someone you give that person access to information that can be used against you. In fact you can be turning over to that person the personal equivalent of the hydrogen bomb, a weapon which can be used to attack your very personhood, the core of what makes you uniquely you. This is why *trust* is a prerequisite of intimacy. And it is why people gradually open up only as trust develops in the total relationship. It is also why self-disclosure (another term for openness) suddenly stops in some relationships. When you discover that information is being used against you, you lose trust, and openness is put on hold.

It is always somewhat amazing to me as a therapist to experience the deep level of trust people have in me within a matter of minutes after meeting me, as compared to the lack of trust they have at that point in their lovers or spouses. It seems that just as intimacy is positively revealed in the degrees of self-disclosure, so it is negatively revealed in the number of secrets we keep from each other. What is particularly sad is the fear people express at the thought of disclosing vital feelings, thoughts, opinions, wishes, and disappointments to one another.

Another essential component of intimacy is confidentiality.

Because of this risk and fear, I will proceed immediately to confidentiality as the next component of intimacy. Because of all that is risked by self-disclosure or openness, it is essential that lovers silently pledge to each other their mutual confidentiality. Lovers must be to each other like priests in a confessional, and look upon the self-disclosures of their beloveds as the most sacred of all trusts, never under any circumstances (even in divorce court) to be revealed.

What I hear in my practice often is the opposite. She shares with the women at the office intimate details of her spouse's self-disclosure about himself.

He makes a joke in public about something that was part of one of their recent sexual experiences. Confidentiality is breached and trust is broken. And as everyone has experienced, once trust is broken it is not quickly regained. Some people, in fact, will never trust completely again. Never! And I do not believe that people can love those they cannot trust.

Therefore a state of confidentiality must be developed over time by people who want a quality intimacy. Little by little we raise the shades and test the confidentiality of the other. Once we experience that it is safe, we will be more courageous and risk even more. Once we discover that our self-disclosures are being shared with others or that they are being used against us, we will quickly pull the shades back down again. It is all the more important, then, for couples to develop with each other that kind of sensitivity which knows when something special, something sacred to another's personhood, is being disclosed and needs to be carefully and confidentially guarded.

After taking a new job, Scott had become very quiet and withdrawn and Velma could not understand why. She asked repeatedly if anything was bothering him, and was assured nothing was wrong. But the silence and withdrawal continued. One night it was so obvious that even Scott could not deny it, and when Velma pleaded with him to tell her, he broke down. In fact he sobbed, something she had never seen him do before. "Velma, I'm just plain scared," he blurted out between sobs. "I was embarrassed to admit that to you. How could you respect a man who was scared he might not live up to the demands of his job?"

Velma just held him, kissed him, and told him she loved him. She assured him he was capable, and that she was not any less admiring of him because he was scared. Scott felt like he'd just had a five-hundred-pound weight lifted off him. Scott's sobs and his fears were never revealed by Velma to anyone.

Commitment is also a component of intimacy.

We experience over time the impossibility of an intimate relationship with someone we are not committed to or with someone not committed to us. In fact, a very crucial ability which we need (part of the sensitivity task in Chapter Five) is the ability to gauge the level of commitment we are getting and giving in a relationship.

I counsel people who have experienced getting hurt time after time in relationships. They complain that they give and give and do not get anything back. People from very dysfunctional families frequently do this—totally commit themselves to people within just a few days or weeks of first meeting them. Too much, too soon.

Healthy relationships have about them a mutuality—"You fill my buckets and I'll fill yours." And so the crucial task here is to gauge the appropriate level of commitment and to give as much as you get. I obviously don't mean that in a strict, literal sense. But it is important to notice when your relationship is definitely lopsided. Both partners should take turns at being lover and "lovee."

Commitment is the will to extend yourself to invest in another, followed by the actions of investment. It is freely wanting to invest in another. It is not guilt induced, not forced in any way. Commitment can only be offered to someone. It cannot be demanded. It should be expected in a good relationship, but it can't be demanded or coerced.

But then the will to love must be followed by the actions of loving (the "bucket filling" as described in Chapter Four). The proof of commitment is not in how many times one says "I love you," but in how well one works at filling the buckets of another.

Another concept that should be discussed here is the concept of fidelity.

Fidelity is *one* way of measuring commitment because real commitment is an exclusive commitment. Let's face it—we have tried "open" relationships and they don't work. And that's not because people are not mature enough or because their self-esteem is too fragile. The fact is that human beings are pair-bonded mammals and so "open" relationships have an almost perfect record of failure.

I have another concern about fidelity, and that is the way we invariably understand it as something we *don't do*—we don't give ourselves to anyone else. Granted it has that negative meaning and action. But fidelity does have a positive side also, a positive action. It ought to, at any rate. My being faithful to you means not only that I won't be with anyone else in this special committed way. It also means that I will always be there *for* you, *when* you need me to be there for you and *in whatever way* you need me to be there.

Janet was furious. She had just spent several days in the hospital recovering from surgery. Alex had missed coming to the hospital two of the eight days she was there, although he did call on those days. Each of those two times he was helping a neighbor and didn't get done in time to make it to the hospital. Now she was furious because he was helping yet another neighbor and had arranged with his sister-in-law to bring Janet home from the hospital. Janet saw a familiar pattern. He could "be there" when others needed him, but never when she did.

I am bothered by the notion that people who have never "fooled around" should trumpet their fidelity when in fact they have not done much of a job of ever "being there" for a beloved or spouse. Nobody should be able to make a self-righteous claim about fidelity without fulfilling both aspects of it.

Finally, equality of power in the relationship is also a component of intimacy.

I am talking here about the necessity of two people approaching each other as equals, in whatever way that is understood and experienced in their culture. This concept is relatively new in human civilization, and still unknown in certain cultures. Most cultures, including our own, have been patriarchal, which is to say men have occupied a superior and women a subordinate position. We have been making rapid strides in America toward a position of full equality for men and women. We are not yet there.

Mel and Ruth each have a demanding career. Both like their careers and both are highly respected by their colleagues. It is a challenge to find quality time together, but they work at it. Neither one demands of the other that one career be sacrificed for the other. They relate to each other as equals. If they don't agree on what movie to see, for instance, they see both of them or take turns choosing. They may not have as much time together as some couples do, but the quality of their relationship is outstanding.

Gary and Mary represent the exact opposite. Gary demands that his fishing and hunting trips take precedence over any other family plans. Yet he considers it an imposition on him when Mary wants to participate in a Christmas shopping trip to Chicago with her cousin and will be gone over one night.

Mel and Ruth experience equality in their relationship. Mary experiences a very frustrating inequality in hers.

There are far better analyses than I can provide of the full picture of equality, of the problems wrought by patriarchal structures of marriage and family, and of the current obstacles to be overcome. There is still a vital and exciting debate about equality. I am indebted to people like Carol Gilligan,[6] Lillian Rubin,[7]

---

6. Carol Gilligan, *In a Different Voice: Psychological Theory and Women's Development* (Cambridge: Harvard University Press, 1982)

7. Lillian Rubin, *Intimate Strangers* (New York: Harper and Row, 1983)

Nancy Chodorow,[8] Arlie Hochschild,[9] Warren Farrell,[10] Herb Goldberg,[11] and others who have brought penetrating insight and illuminating discussion of this complex subject.

All I can say is that one of the laws of intimacy is that people can experience genuine, quality intimacy only as equals. There is something about power that corrupts love. And there is something about love that enables people to become real.

---

8. Nancy Chodorow, *The Reproduction of Mothering: Psychoanalysis and the Sociology of Gender* (Berkeley: University of California Press, 1978)

9. Arlie Hochschild, *The Second Shift* (Avon, NY: Viking, 1989)

10. Warren Farrell, *Why Men Are the Way They Are* (New York: McGraw Hill, 1986)

11. Herb Goldberg, *The Hazards of Being Male* (New York: Signet, 1976)

Chapter 7

❤

Prerequisites for Intimacy

In the previous chapter I outlined the nature and character of intimacy. Intimacy involves the sharing of physical closeness, openness or self-disclosure, commitment, confidentiality, and equal power. Building intimacy or raising the quality of intimacy involves growth in each of those five characteristics.

What growth in intimacy demands, however, is that we have the personal prerequisites. These prerequisites involve some tasks which we must accomplish on our own. It is to be hoped that we will have accomplished these tasks in a previous part of our personal growth or development. But it is clear that people without these prerequisites have problems in relationships.

The first prerequisite is a "differentiated self."

This concept is one of several conceptualized by Murray Bowen, M.D.[1] A person with a well-differentiated self has a healthy sense of "I-ness." As conceptualized by Bowen, there are two major aspects of a differentiated self. The first is our capacity to distinguish between what we think and what we feel. Human beings function as thinking, rational beings, and we function as emotional, feeling beings. Both are important. Both make us human. But we are in trouble when we confuse them.

---

1. Daniel V. Papero, *Bowen Family Systems Theory* (Boston: Allyn and Bacon, 1990)

The truth is that thinking and feeling are confused all the time. Part of the problem, in fact, is language itself. Listen to how often you hear someone say something like, "I feel that we should do more to protect the environment." You see why we have confusion? Doing something to protect the environment is not a "feeling." It's an opinion, a belief, a position—but it's not a feeling. Happy, depressed, outraged, angry, ecstatic—those are feelings. So the first thing we have to do is become more precise with our language. I can give you a simple rule: Whenever you use the word "that" after the verb "feel" you are using "feel" incorrectly. You can "think that" and you can "believe that" but you can't (to be correct) "feel that." Keep that simple rule in your head and you won't easily confuse feelings and thinking.

A self-differentiated person is able to distinguish between feelings and thinking. Nothing in that definition says that both are not important. They are. And actually, one is not more important than the other. People who "don't feel" (actually impossible) or who can't identify their feelings are dangerously out of touch with themselves. I find myself frequently helping people—especially males, and both males and females who were abused as children—get in touch with their feelings. I find myself encouraging people to trust their feelings (as real and genuine) as opposed to distrusting them. I have to do that because so many people have got messages, usually from early caretakers, which invalidated their feelings. They've heard statements like "you don't feel that way," "you shouldn't feel that way," or else they've just been ignored. Males, especially in our culture, are notorious for having a hard time getting in touch with their feelings. We need to get in touch with our feelings again. They are important.

Feelings are important because they are powerful clues to what we are doing that's good for us or bad for us. Powerful clues, but not infallible clues. Positive feelings (e.g., joy, ecstasy) usually indicate to us when we are doing or have done something that's good for us. Negative feelings (e.g., depression, frustration) generally indicate the opposite.

Thinking about what we're doing is necessary to really complete the task of determining the connection between our action and our feeling. We may feel ecstatic but our thinking about it helps us discover, for instance, that learning a new skill contributes to our positive feelings. Likewise, our thinking processes may help us discover what we need to change in our lives to eliminate some frustration or depression.

Thinking is also necessary because our feelings are not always infallible. We may feel "good," but if the ecstasy comes from cocaine we're in trouble. We may feel exhausted and depleted after the hard work of exercising, but our thinking tells us that this is probably good for us anyway.

And then there are those times when our feelings urge us in one direction and our thinking in a different direction. What to do then? Should we follow our heads (thinking) or our hearts? The honest answer to that question is that there is no automatic answer. My bias is that most of the time, when faced with that choice, the better choice is to "go with your head." But the more important truth is to "know what you're doing." If you want to go with your heart then do so—just know you are going with your heart. If that gets you into trouble too often your rational process at some point will probably tell you that in "these" situations you do better when you go with your head and in "those" your are better off to follow your heart. Self-differentiated people don't always follow one or the other, but always know which one they are following.

The other capacity that a self-differentiated person has is the capacity to stay connected to people without being controlled or overwhelmed by the emotional fallout or "reactivity" of others. In a primary sense we are self-differentiated from our family of origin—our parents, siblings, and extended family. As taught by Bowen this self-differentiation is never complete or perfect. It is a matter of degree. And it is pretty fixed until and unless you work with family-of-origin issues to raise your degree of self-differentiation. This is accomplished in therapy through a "coaching" process in which you are assisted in dealing with your original family.

The term "co-dependent" as it is used today comes close to addressing this second aspect of self-differentiation. Although first used in connection with alcoholic families, the term co-dependent has come to be used to describe anyone who for any reason is emotionally reactive to another person to the degree that it adversely affects his or her ability to function as an authentic person, either autonomously or in relationships. Co-dependent people generally have enormous problems establishing or maintaining intimate relationships.

So the first prerequisite for intimacy is to be a differentiated self, a person who integrates feeling and thinking and can stay connected to people without being emotionally reactive to them; a person who can distinguish "what I feel, what I think, what I will do, and what I will not do"—and act on that basis.

Charlene grew up in a "children should be seen and not heard" kind of home. Her father was loud and intimidating. Her mother was quiet and often instructed the children not to do or say something that would upset their father. Charlene can't recall ever hearing her mother express a strong opinion of her own. Charlene hasn't either. She has learned to be a pleaser. When a man asks her out and inquires where she would like to eat she says, "I don't care." The same answer works for which movie she would like to see. She has a hard time buying clothes and has to take someone along who will give her an opinion on what looks good on her. Charlene is not a self-differentiated person.

Leslie is. She has occasional disagreements with her parents about her choices. But she can state clearly and usually calmly what she thinks, what she believes. She feels good when her parents approve but is not deterred when they do not. She maintains the same frequency of contact with her parents regardless of their current approval or disagreement with the decisions she makes. Leslie is a more self-differentiated person.

The second prerequisite is self-esteem.

This probably flows from self-differentiation, but refers more to the worth or value you confer on yourself. And again, as with the prerequisite of self-differentiation, the origin of problems with self-esteem is always in the circumstances of childhood.

The specific circumstance of childhood which creates self-esteem problems more than any other is the dependencies, from absolute to relative, that human children have on adults. I am convinced that even under the best of circumstances we would have problems with self-esteem because of the many years that it takes us to "stand on our own feet." Abuse and dysfunction in families does make that much worse, but even in the case of malicious abuse it is the circumstance of the dependence of the child on the adult that makes the child such a victim.

If you've ever tried to love somebody who has a low self-esteem you know why this is a prerequisite for intimacy. People with low self-esteem cannot believe that they deserve to be esteemed by others. They cannot trust the actions and words of others. They like themselves so little they cannot legitimately ask for what they want or need.

In regard to these first two prerequisites one more observation needs to be made. It is that, almost without exception, people with similar degrees of self-differentiation and similar levels of self-esteem seem to be attracted to each other. Any appearance to the contrary is probably an illusion. This means that finding yourself continually attracted to persons with low self-esteem is a clue that your own self-esteem is probably low. Likewise in regard to self-differentiation. This may also explain why some relationships are doomed when only one partner grows as a person. The similarity is gone and degree of difference just cannot be tolerated. The obvious conclusion is that it is a good idea to work at growing together, to share growth experiences with each other, so that you do not grow widely apart on levels of self-esteem or degrees of self-differentiation.

The third prerequisite is the ability to trust.

Two people in a relationship need to be able to take for granted each other's credibility. Each needs to be able to trust the other's commitment and communication. Trust is something like the foundation or footings of a house. If the footings are not solid nothing above ground will fit together right or be straight. Likewise, in those situations where fundamental, mutual trust is absent the relationship has no foundation.

The proof of the fundamental importance of trust is clear when you experience the consequences of the betrayal of trust.

John confessed to Mary an affair with a neighbor woman. Mary was stunned but indicated to John she would do her best to deal with the matter if he would just be completely open with her. John promised to do just that. He talked about the whole relationship and assured Mary she knew all there was to know. But a few weeks later Mary discovered more. She asked John, "Is that all there is to know now?" He assured her she now knew everything. This pattern continued for several more rounds, however, until whatever trust Mary had in John was completely destroyed.

How do you trust again when someone you trusted betrayed that trust and lied to you? It is very, very difficult. Once trust has been destroyed it can take months, if not years, to rebuild it.

For some people the problem with trust is more of a childhood problem. That is to say, some people have been subjected to such abusive, neglectful, or chaotic childhoods that they learned to survive by trusting nobody. Some children grow up in environments in which there is such severe incongruence between what people say and do, or in environments that are so unpredictable and chaotic, that they never develop a capacity to trust people. These people must learn to trust, must develop some minimal capacity to trust, before they can function well in relationships. This usually means dealing with family-of-origin issues or previous-relationship issues. But you cannot begin to get close to another until you are able to risk trusting. Without that ability self-disclosure is just too threatening. Without trust, anyone can be "the enemy," and all the defensive measures which you take to protect yourself militate against intimacy.

---------------------------- ♥ ----------------------------

The fourth prerequisite for intimacy is the ability to withstand criticism.

While we all would like to find relationships in which we experience unconditional love and approval, it is not likely to happen. We are bound to make some mistakes, even with the best of intentions. And no matter how hard we try we will not accomplish perfection.

I am assuming that the kind of criticizing that is done in a healthy relationship is not the "personal attack" variety—remarks like "You're stupid." "You can't do anything right." That's not criticism. That's abuse. And no one has to tolerate abuse.

I am talking about what is often referred to as "constructive criticism," that is, criticism given to help one to grow or improve rather than to attack and belittle. Personally, I believe even "constructive criticism" hurts. But it is still sometimes necessary.

People whose personal sense of security is so fragile that even the slightest imperfection devastates them have real problems in relationships. The slightest mistake makes them feel totally worthless and incompetent. I am reminded of that delightful observation in *The Velveteen Rabbit* by Margery Williams[2] in which she suggests that people who have to be "too carefully kept" do not experience the real closeness of a loving relationship. To demand perfection of your-

---

2. Margery Williams, *The Velveteen Rabbit* (New York: Bianco Publishing, 1922)

self is to demand too much. To expect another, especially one who is close to you, to see you only as perfect and faultless is unrealistic and impossible.

The fifth prerequisite for intimacy is "time together alone."

The final observation I would make about intimacy is to stress the prerequisite of "time together alone," or "sacred time" as I call it. Couples must really make the time in their lives to be together alone. This needs to be done daily and weekly because these are the intervals by which we arrange our lives. I believe these times together alone must be consciously negotiated and planned or they will not happen as regularly as they should. For better or for worse we arrange our lives into schedules, routines, and habitual patterns. Therefore we need to schedule the time to be together. The evidence points solidly to the fact that when that is not done and people count on just catching time together when they can, they just don't find enough time together alone. And then slowly they just drift apart.

I suggest to almost all the couples I work with that they negotiate a daily period of time to consist of a minimum of thirty minutes when they will be together alone. It is the honoring of this time as well as the time itself which has a positive benefit. Then I ask them to also negotiate a weekly period of time consisting of at least two hours when they will be together alone *away from the home or apartment.* And finally, I suggest they make a commitment to each other to spend the better part of a weekend away together alone every two or three months.

It is in these periods of time together alone that people can fill each other's buckets. And more than that, when each partner honors the commitment of these times together the other experiences a feeling of specialness.

Chapter 8

Love and Conflict

"If it don't come easy better let it go," is a line in a country western song.[1] The song is talking about love and relationships. I have ambivalent reactions to the notion that love should come "easy."

The first reaction is that nothing in life that is worthwhile comes easy. As I said in Chapter Three, the truth about love is that it takes work—enjoyable work I would hope, but work nonetheless. Part of that work has to do with conflict. Conflict is a normal phenomenon in a relationship. It is to be expected. It is not a sign (of itself) that the relationship is in big trouble or is in any way dysfunctional.

Yet I have another reaction to that line from the song. I think there is something true about it. If it isn't ever "easy" to negotiate with a lover, there is something wrong. If the relationship is just one long continuous series of conflicts, there most certainly is a problem. If one person is always afraid to speak frankly because the other person will be hurt or angry, distance will result. It should be easy to speak your own point of view. You should always be able to do so without fearing the other person will "lose it." If that isn't easy, you have a problem. It means that you are in a relationship that cannot deal with conflict.

There are some patterns of conflict which indicate that something is seriously wrong. The first is when you notice you are having the same conflict over and over. In other words, the conflict is not being resolved. That's a big warning sign which should point you to some outside help.

---

1. Gibson and Kemp, "If It Don't Come Easy"

Another warning sign is when one party either walks out and remains gone for some time, or doesn't talk for a period of time, sometimes days. Another sign, obviously, is when either one is quickly at the brink of violence.

Having made the point that conflict is normal within certain limits, let me offer some suggestions or strategies for handling and resolving conflict. These suggestions may be thought of as seven rules.

Rule One: Make sure you are both having the same conflict.

Both need to be clear as to what the issue is.

Rule Two: Make sure you each find out the position of the other in relationship to the issue.

Make sure you hear each other. I sometimes have partners in a couple contract with each other to go through an exercise in which one person expresses a view and the other must first say, "What I hear you saying is _____ ." If the original speaker says yes to that restatement of the view the second person may then state a position. If the answer is no the first speaker must say it again. This exercise merely forces people to hear each other and prevents one from *assuming* knowledge of what the other is thinking, believing, or feeling.

Rule Three: Have one conflict at a time.

I have heard something like the following in my office many times:

He: I'm getting sick and tired of coming home to a trashed-out house. When are you going to learn to be a decent housekeeper?

She: Maybe I'd be a better housekeeper if I ever knew when you were coming home—and that when you got home you'd do something besides sit in the living room with your evening drink!

He: I don't need any remarks from you about my drinking, not when your mother drinks the way she does.

She: I suppose you prefer the way your mother comes over here and rearranges the furniture without even asking.

And on, and on . . .

These two people are having several conflicts at once. As a result, none of them will be settled. We must resist the tendency to shift the conflict, a tendency no doubt related to our sense that we will have a better chance to win if we shift to one that we are pretty sure we can win.

Rule Four: Don't get personal!

Personal attacks on the other's appearance, intelligence, or personhood are abusive. Remarks like those do not fill that respect bucket, but kick it instead.

He: I don't like it when you yell at the kids like that.
She: I don't need any advice from someone not smart
enough to finish the eighth grade.

**Rule Five: Both need to enter into and
carry on the conflict with a commitment
that both can come out winners instead
of one a winner and one a loser.**

Demands for unconditional surrender create bad
feelings. Lovers should not want to or enjoy playing
winners and losers.

**Rule Six: Ask each other, "How could we
do things differently so we don't have to
have this particular conflict again?"**

I believe it helps if somewhere in the middle of
the conflict each assumes equal responsibility for
putting this question on the table. I'm not trying to
suggest that all conflict will be eliminated. That's
impossible. But lots of conflicts, specific and individual ones, could be eliminated by doing something
different.

For example, one couple argued every night
about when to eat dinner. He came home from work
any time between 5:15 and 7:30 p.m. It was quickly
determined, however, that by 3:30 almost any day he
could know when he would be getting home. The
couple decided to have phone contact at 3:30 each
day to eliminate the confusion and uncertainty. It was

agreed that he would fix dinner on the night he could get home before 6:00 and she would fix dinner on the other nights, or they would decide to eat out.

Another couple settled an argument about never having time together by agreeing that they would each keep certain blocks of time for activities together and not commit themselves to any activities, including social invitations, without checking with each other.

Rule Seven: Be willing to admit a mistake.

Everybody makes mistakes. You should not demand perfection of yourself or of your lover. A simple "I'm sorry," if sincere, will go a long way.

Conflicts arise out of the differences that exist among people. We have different points of view, different opinions, different likes and dislikes. We often experience these differences as something wrong with our relationship.

I would like to suggest another way of looking at our differences. We can also think of differences as providing balance to a relationship. Our differences then can be a way of preventing imbalance.

For example, one person is inclined to make decisions impulsively; the other to be cautious and thoughtful. Together they provide a balance, each one contributing his or her own characteristics in a way that prevents either an impulsive pattern or a "we better not" pattern from becoming the rut in which the relationship founders.

Most couples whom I know represent in their relationship that kind of balance created by their differences. One partner is more a spender, the other more a saver of money; one stricter, the other more permissive in regard to child discipline; one more, the other less social or outgoing; one talkative, the other quiet. Some authorities believe that we are attracted to one another more on the basis of our differences than our similarities. Our personality characteristics complement each other.

That truth may help us give up the notion that our relationships would be so much better if the other person were just "more like me." I'm suggesting that we simply learn to re-frame our differences as a strength rather than a weakness in our relationships.

It also needs to be said, however, that some kinds of difference are indeed serious because they are fundamental and incompatible differences. More than differences in personality, they are philosophical in nature. They have more to do with our vision of life—how we shape and envision our own life journeys.

In an earlier chapter I wrote about the necessity for all of us to have our own orbits. Included in each orbit is our sense of an individual past, present, and future; some sense of vocation or calling for our lives. I am talking now of a particular world view through which we each make sense of that individual past and which gives direction for the future. People with incompatible philosophies of life are dealing with differences which cannot be resolved by discussion or conflict. The best such persons will ever be able to do is agree to disagree.

The truth is that people with such fundamental differences are not often even attracted to each other. But sometimes they wind up in a relationship anyway.

They may do so because they do not really articulate their philosophies until much later. Or they may be pushed by their physical attraction and passion into ignoring their fundamental differences. And sometimes people grow in such a way as to move from one philosophical position to another.

This is why major differences in culture, religion, and ethnic background are so important—because *sometimes* these differences involve major differences in one's world view. What is at issue is not personality characteristics but our views of such basic concepts as manhood, womanhood, the purpose and meaning of existence, or human nature. Differences in these areas lead to serious distances between people.

I am not suggesting for a minute that people of different religions, races, or ethnic backgrounds cannot marry. I am saying that they need to explore how their own individual religions, races, or ethnic backgrounds have shaped their world views. Skin color is of little significance. Whether one actively strives against the harsh realities of human existence or passively accepts them is of great significance. Likewise, whether one prefers a church experience that is highly liturgical and rich in symbol or one that is quite unstructured and without symbol is of moderately serious importance; whether one is permitted to have a blood transfusion in a life-threatening situation is of much greater importance.

A fairly simple test for the partners in any couple to give themselves is to ask whether their differences are merely matters of style, taste, or backgrounds, or whether they are matters of fundamental beliefs about issues like God or human nature. The latter issues do not lend themselves to negotiation and compromise because they have to do with basic and fundamental beliefs that shape how we think about the world and our lives in the world.

A Final Word

It is clear that we are living in a time of transition as far as marriage and family are concerned. A new consciousness has been developing about womanhood for some time now. There are signs that a new consciousness about manhood is also beginning to develop, at least here in the United States.

Just as individual growth periods of transition are marked with intense feelings and behavioral symptoms (the "terrible two's" and adolescence) so cultural transitions and social patterns of marriage and family may be shaky and even seem chaotic. The truth is that we are demanding much more of our marriages and erotic relationships than our grandparents did—much more.

We are asking ourselves to create relationships which endure for a lifetime but which maintain a high quality of intimacy throughout. We are asking ourselves as couples to maneuver through the honeymoon stage, child raising, child launching, retirement, and old age without compromising quality intimacy and friendship. We are asking ourselves as couples to spend fifty years and more together, each partner managing to pursue an individual life orbit but managing as a couple to steer them in such a way that they overlap sufficiently for each to be able to experience being well loved. We are asking ourselves, as we meet the challenges of changing careers, changing health, and changing technology, to manage to fill for each other on a daily basis the buckets of attention, recognition, respect, affection, and separateness.

Are we, in fact, asking too much? Some of my friends and colleagues believe the answer is clearly *yes.* We cannot expect all that out of one relationship. There are quite serious and responsible people who are suggesting that today's divorce rate is evidence for the fact that we may need two or three relationships through a lifetime as we change or grow.

Perhaps. Still I see couples who have managed to get through all the stages and challenges of life and who have managed to develop a vital, rich, and satisfying intimacy. The form and style of their relationship may have changed many times but the substance has always been there. They have had their conflicts, even severe ones, but they have endured.

I have always liked Erich Fromm's title, *The Art of Loving.*[1] Is that not finally what it is all about? Loving, like living itself, is an art—to be learned, to be cultivated, to be practiced, to be developed and transformed. Our mistake is in assuming that we can just skim the beginners book and become "concert" lovers. It takes constant practice. It takes discipline. It takes willingness to study new techniques. But when all is said and done, perhaps the real test of any person or any society is how well that person or society has mastered the art of loving.

---

1. Fromm, *Art of Loving*

Bibliography

Bradshaw, John. *Homecoming*. New York: Bantam, 1990.

Browning, Elizabeth Barrett. *Sonnets from the Portuguese*.

Buscaglia, Leo. *Love*. Greenwich: Fawcett, 1972.

Choderow, Nancy. *The Reproduction of Mothering: Psychoanalysis and the Sociology of Gender*. Berkeley: University of California Press, 1978.

Farrell, Warren. *Why Men Are the Way They Are*. New York: McGraw Hill, 1986.

Fromm, Erich. *The Art of Loving*. New York: Harper and Row, 1956.

Gilligan, Carol. *In a Different Voice: Psychological Theory and Women's Development*. Cambridge: Harvard University Press, 1982.

Glasser, William. *Control Theory*. New York: Harper and Row, 1984.

Goldberg, Herb. *The Hazards of Being Male*. New York: Signet, 1976.

Hendrix, Harville. *Getting the Love You Want*. New York: Henry Holt and Company, 1988.

Hochschild, Arlie. *The Second Shift*. Avon, NY: Viking, 1989.

Mace, David. *We Can Have Better Marriages*. Nashville, TN: Abingdon, 1974.

Napier, Augustus. *The Fragile Bond*. New York: Harper and Row, 1988.

Papero, Daniel V. *Bowen Family Systems Theory*. Boston: Allyn and Bacon, 1990.

Powell, John, S.J. *Why Am I Afraid to Tell You Who I Am?* Allen, TX: Tabor Publishing, a division of DLM, Inc., 1969.

Rosin, Mark Bruce. *Stepfathering*. New York: Simon and Schuster, 1987.

Rubin, Lillian. *Intimate Strangers*. New York: Harper and Row, 1983.

Textor, Martin, ed. *The Divorce and Divorce Therapy Handbook*. Northvale, NJ: J. Aronson, Inc., 1989.

Wallerstein, Judith, et al. *Surviving the Breakup*. New York: Harper Torch Books, 1980.

Williams, Margery. *The Velveteen Rabbit*. New York: Bianco Publishing, 1922.

About the Author

A marriage and family counselor of many years' varied experience, Richard Osing is uniquely qualified as the author of *How to Love and Be Loved*. A counselor since 1986 at the Neuropsychiatric Clinic in Iowa City, Iowa, he specializes in marital, family, and divorce therapy; step-family dynamics; and individual counseling for life-adjustment problems. He spent several years as Executive Director of Foundation II, a crisis-intervention program for runaway children, suicide intervention, and spouse and child abuse; also as Executive Director of the Council on Aging, dealing with assessment and intervention for the elderly and their families. He was also a high school counselor, and a parish minister for nearly twenty years.

Mr. Osing's professional training includes undergraduate and graduate degrees from Concordia College and Concordia Seminary in St. Louis, and post-graduate courses in his field from several colleges and universities, as well as extensive clinical training.

He is the author of two published articles and a videotape, and has given many workshops and seminars on step-family relations, divorce adjustment, self-esteem, and family dynamics.

Will Dick Osing speak to my group or organization?

The answer is Yes! Throughout Dick's career, he has given hundreds of presentations on a variety of topics. In fact, the popularity of his presentation on Love and Relationships was one of the contributing factors that influenced him to write this book. Dick's audiences range in size from hundreds to a few dozen, and have included national conferences and seminars, State Department of Corrections, community colleges, health-care professionals, church groups, and high school classes, among others.

The following is a list of topics that Dick has covered in the past:

How to Love and Be Loved
Raising the Quality of Intimacy
Living and Loving in Remarried Families
Love and Marriage at Mid-Life
The Dual-Career Couple
Parenting (General Principles)
Parenting Teen-agers
Depression and Marriage
How to Raise Your Self-Esteem
Healing Strategies for Dysfunctional Families
Life After Divorce—The Healing Process
New Models of Masculinity

If your group or organization is looking for a speaker for a meeting, seminar, or conference, and would like to consider Dick, please contact:

The Consortium Corporation
c/o Steven L. Fairchild
P.O. Box 2419
Cedar Rapids, Iowa 52406
319-399-6901
1-800-999-6901

Richard A. Osing
cordially invites you to share
How to Love and Be Loved
with a friend

To order, please complete this form and send it to The Consortium Corporation, Publishing Division, P.O. Box 2419, Cedar Rapids, IA 52406. To order by phone (credit card orders only) call 319-399-6901 or 1-800-999-6901. Please allow 2–4 weeks for delivery.

Name _____

Address _____

City_____ **State** ____ **Zip** _____

Number of copies _____ ($11.95 per copy) $ _____

Sales tax (Iowa residents only) $ _____

Shipping and handling $ 2.50

Total cost $ _____

☐ Check or money order
☐ MasterCard
☐ VISA

Credit card number: ⎢⎢⎢⎢⎢⎢⎢⎢⎢⎢⎢⎢⎢⎢⎢⎢⎢⎢⎢

Expiration date: ⎢⎢⎢⎢⎢⎢

Cardholder's signature: _____

Please do not send cash. Make checks payable to The Consortium Corporation. Your check will be deposited upon receipt. Credit card payment will be charged to your account upon shipment of your order.   Form 1915

Richard A. Osing
cordially invites you to share
How to Love and Be Loved
with a friend

To order, please complete this form and send it to The Consortium Corporation, Publishing Division, P.O. Box 2419, Cedar Rapids, IA 52406. To order by phone (credit card orders only) call 319-399-6901 or 1-800-999-6901. Please allow 2–4 weeks for delivery.

Name _____

Address _____

City_____ **State** ____ **Zip** _____

Number of copies _____ ($11.95 per copy) $ _____

Sales tax (Iowa residents only) $ _____

Shipping and handling $ 2.50

Total cost $ _____

☐ Check or money order
☐ MasterCard
☐ VISA

Credit card number: └┴┴┴┴┴┴┴┴┴┴┴┴┴┴┴┴┴┴┘

Expiration date: └┴┴┴┴┘

Cardholder's signature: _____

Please do not send cash. Make checks payable to The Consortium Corporation. Your check will be deposited upon receipt. Credit card payment will be charged to your account upon shipment of your order.   Form 1915